EVERTON GREATS:

WHERE ARE THEY NOW?

MAINSTREAM SPORT

EVERTON GREATS

WHERE ARE THEY NOW?

JON BERMAN AND MALCOLM DOME

MAINSTREAM
PUBLISHING

EDINBURGH AND LONDON

First published in Great Britain in 1997 by
MAINSTREAM PUBLISHING COMPANY (EDINBURGH) LTD
7 Albany Street
Edinburgh EH1 3UG

ISBN 1 84018 805 7

Revised and updated, 2003

A catalogue record for this book is available from the British Library

Typeset in Times
Printed and bound in Great Britain by Cox & Wyman Ltd

This book is dedicated to the late Leila Berman.

A mother watching over.

Contents

Acknowledgements

Thanks? Of course, both of us want to thank every player who took the time and trouble to talk to us, treating us with a courtesy that was truly humbling. Top of the list must be Brian Labone, who made such an important contribution to making this book possible. Brian was once described by no less a person than Harry Catterick as 'The Last of the Corinthians'. And he has held us in thrall on so many occasions, with his exuberance and enthusiasm for the club, that both of us still feel we have to pinch ourselves to realise an Everton giant would even give us the time of day. Sir, you are a gentleman.

Oh, and strange as it may seem, we must also thank two people connected with (would you believe it!) Liverpool – Mike Walker (no relation to our old manager) and Phil Thompson. Despite the fact that their allegiances lie on the wrong side of Stanley Park, both were exceptionally helpful as we tried to track down one or two players who seemed to have disappeared off the face of the earth. They may be red, but they're good chaps anyway.

Malcolm would like to thank Sharon Black, Annick Barbaria, the *TotalRock* crew, Xavier Russell, Dave Ling, Jerry Ewing, too many great rock bands to mention and the CroBar in London's West End, not an Everton hang-out, but a great place nonetheless. Oh yes, I could not forget one other person, Steve McTaggart (told you I'd embarrass you by putting you in an Everton book).

Jon would like to thank the following people, without whom this book would never have seen the light of day. (Anyway, if he doesn't thank them they have threatened to take away his Everton memorabilia and his e-mail facility!) They are:

Steve Brooker, Travis Benson, Anthony Williams, Frank Williams, Erling Antoni Saevik, Nick Bratt, Steve Malone, Joe Hannah, Enza Santangelo, Barry Honey, Edric Sng, Harjinder, Kevin McGoverin, Ciaran Meegan, Darryl Ng, James Goddard, Martin Lindland, Matt Traynor, David Catton, Wayne Hughes, John Bracken, Kevin Hazard, Robert

Sharratt, Lauren Hazard, Yusuf Kay, Mark Paddy Weston, Gerard O'Connor, Tony Lloyd, David Ellis, Julian Jackson, Martin Smith, Edric, Stan Nuttall, Philip Bowker, Ken Myers, Andrew Pritchard, Nigel Cunliffe, Dave Davies, Nicholas Gard, Keith Giles, Alan Stoops, Justin Campbell, Elaine Berman, Jimmy Tan Hua Seng, Melanie Berman, Linda Borregales, Danielle Berman, Lol Scragg, Tracey Nordemann, Lawrence Noel Breakey, Michi Nordemann, Mark Roberts, Sarah Nordemann, Phil Roberts, Jason Nordemann, Jon Duffy, Ken Doughty, Dr Paul Preston, Steve Hulse, Sid Preston, David Galbraith (East Fife Rule!), Andrea Thrussell, Melville Berman (Father and a True Blue), Clive Blackmore and Ray Simpson (Burnley FC Historian).

Foreword

So, whatever did become of what's his name . . .

When we started out on this project, we had one aim in mind: to talk to some of the great names from Everton's past, coax out of them memories of their time at Goodison and to find out just what happened to them after they left the club. The two of us didn't want to talk to loads of players and just write a few lines on each; we really wanted a chance to select the players and talk to them in depth, giving them the space and respect their contributions to the club's history deserved.

So, we drew up a short list and started to track them down. Some were easy. Others not so easy. Some were very talkative. Others a little more difficult.

We had two criteria for the term 'great': either players who were part of a great team, or those who were memorable stars in underachieving teams. Of course, some of the former were wonderful players in their own right anyway. Others may not have been world class, yet still made a contribution. You can argue the toss about some of the names we've included and wonder about the absence of others, but we never set out to write about every single player who ever wore the royal blue shirt. What do you want: *Encyclopedia Evertonia*?

All the players included here left their mark on Everton in one way or another, and between them they cover the last 50 years of the club, and therein lies the bonus that we never expected. In a sense what you have here is the history of Everton Football Club, from just after the Second World War right up to the present day, but told through the eyes of the people who made it all happen: the players. At times their anecdotes and opinions provide conflicting evidence on situations, managers and eras. But there is stuff in here that you will probably have never come across before.

Just why did Alan Ball leave the club for Arsenal, one of the most perplexing transfer deals in Everton's history? We think we may have got to the truth through talking to some of his Everton contemporaries.

Was Gordon Lee a managerial disaster, as most Everton fans old enough to recall his reign at the club from 1977 until 1981 have always believed? Perhaps after reading what his players have to say you will, like us, start to revise your attitude.

How good a manager was Harry Catterick? How did the players view him? Why did he allow the great 1970 championship-winning side to fall apart? You may be surprised by what you read here.

Billy Bingham. Johnny Carey. Ian Buchan. Cliff Britton. Howard Kendall. Their managerial acumen is dissected and discussed, and in some cases the evidence backs up the reputation. In others . . . well, let's just say you might be somewhat amazed at what comes out.

We do not lay claim to have written a definitive history of Everton – well that was never the intention anyway. But we feel that, while you will be interested in the individual players as heroes and human beings, we have come up with a book that gives an original slant on the development of the club. What comes across more than anything else is the affection in which all the players we spoke to still hold the club. They still care about what happens at L4 4EL. Like all of us who follow the Blues, they have been bitten by the bug, and there is no antidote – thank goodness.

We went into this book looking forward idealistically to speaking to heroes and legends, but fearful that the real people behind these stories and statistics may turn out to be men of straw. We discovered titans who more than lived up to our expectations, boyhood idols who will forever remain golden gods in their prime, and who did nothing to diminish their iconic status during the interviews we conducted for the book.

Finally, this book is all about an illogical passion: it frustrates us, annoys us, often leaves us in despair and seething with rage, but goddammit we can't help it. Everton Football Club, what would we do without you!

Introduction

It's often said: once an Evertonian, always an Evertonian. And that applies as much to players as fans.

I've been associated with this great club now for more than 40 years. I started out as a fan, cheering on my heroes from the terraces, before being privileged to pull on the royal blue jersey and play for the club for a number of years. I was lucky enough to captain Everton as we lifted the FA Cup and League Championship trophy in 1966 and 1970, respectively. And, even though I've long since retired from the playing side, I remain involved with them – and I can tell you that being associated with Everton still gives me a real buzz.

From my many years connected with Goodison, I know just how much the club means to players, whether they've been here for a brief period or enjoyed a lengthy stay. It gets in your blood and stays there. In fact, I know of no other club that generates this lifelong affection among former players. Why? I don't know. There's just something special about the place and, of course, something unique about the fans who follow our fortunes around the world.

When Jon Berman and Malcolm Dome approached me to help them with this book, I was, naturally, delighted. Not only at the opportunity to help two obviously genuine Evertonians in their labour of love, but also to help bring back to the forefront the names of players who contributed so much in their time at the club, but who history hasn't perhaps treated as kindly as it might. Evertonians don't forget about their heroes, but sometimes it's good to be reminded not only of their exploits, but also about them as human beings.

For some of you, this will bring back memories – happy and maybe not-so-happy – of past seasons. For others, it will offer the chance to discover part of the rich heritage of Everton FC.

Whatever, enjoy the book and keep supporting the team.

Best wishes

Brian Labone

CHAPTER ONE

Alan Ball

EVERTON PLAYING CAREER:1966–1971
GAMES PLAYED: 249
GOALS SCORED: 78

If there is one player in the modern history of Everton Football Club who epitomised a winner, it's got to be Alan Ball. Alan was the one that every Everton fan looked to, when he was on the pitch, to show a flash of genius that would lead to a goal. His competitive streak was legendary. His fiery nature on the pitch excited the Everton fans. Alan Ball wanted to be second to no one. Looking back today, Alan must be regarded as one of the all-time Everton heroes. A few weeks after the world saw Alan and Nobby Stiles dancing round the Wembley pitch after winning the World Cup in 1966, Harry Catterick signed up this precocious talent that would help take the club to a Championship win four years later. To think that Everton might have lost out to their big Yorkshire rivals, Leeds United, in getting his signature.

I heard that Everton were interested in me, one day after a training session at Blackpool, through a phone call from Ron Suart, the manager. He wanted me to go back to the ground to speak to me. When I got there, he informed me that there was interest from both Everton and Leeds United. They both offered the same money for me and it was up to me to make my choice. The thing that swung it for me in joining Everton was that I didn't have to leave home. It was just down the East Lancs road and I would rather do that than live in Leeds.

Everton paid Blackpool £110,000, a British transfer record at the time, to have a player who only weeks earlier had played an important part in English football history.

Well, it was a busy summer for me. I had played in the World Cup final at Wembley and I was transferred to Everton. The World Cup was incredible. Like most 21 year olds, I looked upon the game as a very important one, but I didn't realise the significance of it until the final whistle. I was just taking each game as it came and going from one result to another and I thought what was all the fuss about. Then it sunk in what we had achieved. It was an amazing match with all the highs and lows. The build-up to it was exciting. It was what everybody in England wanted. It was something that had never been done before and of course it hasn't been repeated.

The fact that after the World Cup, Everton came in for me didn't faze me at all. I was naturally confident anyway in my abilities as a player. The World Cup helped me handle those types of things like being a bigger name in football. I had, after all, had the honour of being one of 11 players in England to win a World Cup-winners' medal.

To say that Alan had a good start to his Everton career would be a major understatement. He scored on his full début, which turned out to be the winning goal, against Fulham at Craven Cottage on the opening day of the 1966–67 season. Then two weeks later he lined up against Liverpool at Goodison Park for a taste of his first derby match. He soon felt at home as he scored two goals in a 3–1 win.

To score on my début was a great feeling. It was a good goal. I had the fans on my side. It was marvellous. Then to follow it up with two against Liverpool – I couldn't have had a greater start. I was still only 21 years old and I, like a lot of fans, had my heroes, people like Dennis Stevens, Alex Young, Fred Pickering and Roy Vernon who were there at the time. Only a couple of years before, I had been reading about them in magazines and newspapers. Now, here I was playing and training with them. However, I was not overawed by them as I knew the likes of Ray Wilson from the World Cup, and I also had confidence in my own ability. I was just pleased that the supporters took to me just like they had done with the others and I felt at home immediately.

Alan settled in very quickly. He forged good relationships with Howard Kendall and Colin Harvey, his midfield partners who, with Alan, were to become probably the best midfield trio in British football.

Manager Harry Catterick, however, was found to be someone who was not the personal type when it came to dealing with players.

Harry managed from afar. He was very much a discipline and fear man. The longer I was there, the more I learned not to take too much to heart somebody who ruled by fear. It was all part of growing up and I reckon that because he ruled by fear, that that was the reason he changed the teams around as often as he did. The reason in my opinion was that the bark would have lost that little bit of bite with the more successful players because we had proved ourselves.

We had a very fit side at Everton, but by the same token we had an awful lot of very good players. Over the years, in football, very good players don't take to a lot of training. They are like good horses. They pace themselves. Wilf Dixon trained us very hard. We were as fit as anyone that I have ever come across in the game. Mind you we were all young lads competing against each other to get into the team, so we didn't need as much to get us fit.

We were very close as a group of players. As a lot of people know, I was a bit of a wild thing at that time and one person that gave me great advice and took me under his wing, so to speak, was Alex Young. When I look back it was like a family. We got on with each other very well. Howard, Colin and myself transported that understanding onto the pitch. I still see some of the players from time to time. I come across the lads often when I do the odd bit of television and so on.

Even winners like Alan have to go through the bad times. There were none greater than in 1968 in the FA Cup final against West Bromwich Albion.

We couldn't believe how much possession we had that day. The only thing we needed was a bit of luck. We were playing the whole match in their half. We missed so many chances. I wouldn't mind but we had beaten them that season 6–2 at the Hawthorns, and we had beaten them at home as well. We went to Wembley very confident that we would score against them but we kept missing the chances. I've never seen a more one-sided cup final where the better team lost. I wouldn't mind but the goal was a fluke as well. For me personally to have got to Wembley three times in my career and not come away with a winners' medal is very disappointing. Having said that, people play all their lives and never get to play at Wembley once, so really it was not all bad.

In the 1969–70 season, Alan achieved, along with the others, the highest honour in winning a championship medal. Everton won the championship quite comfortably in the end. For Alan, it was that much more personal in terms of satisfaction.

It was a great achievement winning in the style that we did. For me it was extra special. Brian Labone was injured towards the end of that season and Harry gave me the captaincy. Once we had seen off the challenge by Leeds United at around Easter time, we won the league fairly comfortably. I think we won it by seven or eight points in the end, which was an incredible margin to win it by considering the amount of very good teams in the league. There was no doubt, though, that we were by far and away the best team in England. For me to be captain at the time when we won the league was extra special. I was so proud to have lifted that trophy. The night we clinched the Championship, against West Brom, I got home very late. We went into town and had a great time. The bond between the club and the supporters ensured that it was that little bit extra special. I felt that at that time we had probably had the edge over Liverpool for the last four seasons anyway.

I was playing with some all-time greats in that era. People like Best, Law and Charlton at Manchester United. Tottenham had great players like Mackay and so on. There were stars in nearly every team in the first division at that time. It was a wonderful period in English football.

Following the winning of the league, Everton seemed to lose their way. They did not seem to be able to build on the success that they had fought so hard to achieve. For everyone concerned it was puzzling.

I've thought long and hard about why we never built on that success. I suppose I can liken it to having a puppy. You smack it when it's young to train it to do the things that you want it to do, but in the end it bites back because it has wised up. Once that had happened with the players, I think Harry decided to change things around very quickly. He was well known for that. He didn't seem to like the fact that players were standing on their own two feet and thinking for themselves, so he just changed teams. That was his method of managing.

In 1971, the biggest bombshell to hit the Everton fans was that their beloved midfield maestro was sold to Arsenal. It is well known that Alan had not wanted to go. It was also well known that the day Alan left Everton, there were a lot of broken hearts to be mended. The transfer took place in November and it was done very quickly indeed. It would be a long time before Everton was to be graced with the presence of such a player. Harry had said all along that Alan was not for sale. He was even quoted as saying that it would take a bid of around £1 million before Everton would even consider selling him. So it was a major shock when it was announced he was going.

I just went into training one day and Harry called me into his office where he told me that Arsenal had tabled a bid of £220,000, which was a British record. The board had accepted the bid. I told him that I didn't want to go. What I couldn't understand was that I was captain of his team and I was playing for England, so I asked him why he wanted to let me go. He said that it was good business for the club. He said that he had had me for six years and that he would be making a profit of £110,000 and that he was doubling his money and therefore it made good business sense. Football was and is a business. Bertie Mee was in the other room waiting to speak to me. I just knew I had to go then and everything was settled quickly. It still didn't make sense to me, but that's football. Mind you I was joining the team that had won the double and they were a very good side.

Alan appeared 177 times for Arsenal and still played with the passion that Everton fans knew from old. However, Alan didn't win any honours with Arsenal and that is something that he still rues.

I was involved in all sorts of great games for Arsenal. I enjoyed it down in London. We challenged on all fronts for about three or four seasons. I'm just sorry that I didn't win any medals for them, but we got beaten in cup finals, we were runners up in the league twice and we got beat in semi-finals. It was just one of those periods in my life where I never won anything, which was disappointing.

Alan's next stop was at Southampton in the 1976–77 season. His departure seemed to be as sudden as when he left Everton.

I came into work and I was told that Lawrie McMenemy had made an offer for me and that I could go if I wanted. Well, you always go when you are not wanted. I joined them for about £60,000. They were in the second division at that time. I joined them just after Christmas and by the end of the season we were promoted back into the first, so that was nice to be able to help them achieve that.

Alan was by now coming to the end of his career as a player, and he was offered the chance to move to America. Like a lot of the top players who were beginning to think about finishing their careers, Alan moved there and found that some of the all-time greats were plying their trade with a newer audience.

When I went out there, the types of players that were there were players that I think most fans loved to see. There was Pelé and Carlos Alberto from Brazil; Cruyff, Neeskens, Rudi Krol from Holland and Peter Osgood, the ex-Chelsea player. There were lots of others. It was a very exciting time. I went to see if I could help Vancouver Whitecaps to win the Soccer Bowl and be champions of North America, beating the great Cosmos and people like that. That was another highlight of my career and I enjoyed that. I was playing out there in the summer and then I would come back to play in England during the winter. I felt that because of my age, I should be playing all year round rather than playing for six months and then having to go through the pre-season to try and get fit for a season.

In the 1980–81 season, Alan came back to Blackpool where he started his career. He was made player-manager. He readily acknowledges that he wasn't ready for management at that time, and that it was a mistake and he didn't do a very good job whilst he was there. After this brief flirtation with management, Alan ended up back at Southampton playing again. He was only meant to be used as a squad player but his form was good enough that he played for another two seasons.

I enjoyed my time at Southampton. Lawrie was a very good man-manager. He bought a lot of good players. He gelled us all together and we won a lot of games for him. I kept myself as fit as I could, and I played in Hong Kong after that for a summer and then went to Bristol Rovers for a short spell.

By now, Alan was approaching 40 years of age and he soon started to think again about management. He had had a fantastic career and he wanted to go into management properly. Looking back on his career at Everton there were some memorable goals and games. The two most disappointing things to have happened to him while he was at Everton were that he never won a cup-winners' medal, and secondly being told that he was being sold, much against his will.

There were dozens of games that were marvellous games. The goal against Liverpool in the cup-tie that put us through into the sixth round in the 1966–67 season has to have been one of the most memorable games. They had the screens up at Anfield for that one. The two goals against Liverpool in my first derby were something special for me as the fans really took to me, and the other goal I look back on was my début goal for the club against Fulham. There's been so many great times and great games associated with Everton.

Portsmouth provided the platform for him to learn the ropes. He had wanted to start off as youth-team coach and learn about all aspects of a football club. He was there as youth-team coach for two years until Bobby Campbell was sacked. Alan was promoted and the club enjoyed a good spell for four years. They just missed out on promotion but they had a very consistent position in the league, being third or fourth for most of the time. Then for the first time in 36 years, Portsmouth got themselves promoted to the first division, and Alan thought that he could take on most things to do with management. He left Portsmouth and took over at Stoke halfway through the 1989–90 season.

I took over and I was expected to perform miracles with little or no money. The players were not good enough, but you take the job and you do your very best to make something good happen. I couldn't turn it round at Stoke. There was one game which we had lost and I went to the chairman and told him that the job was not for me and that I felt I was letting myself down, and everybody else, and that I wanted to be released from my contract. Fortunately, I only had a short contract and the chairman agreed and so I left. I then ended up at Exeter City for three wonderful years. That was a different type of situation. We did OK as a team, and financially I made £75,000 for them one year and it was something that had never happened before. To them that meant it had been a successful season. That's the sort of thing that puts it all into perspective.

Then the chance to rejoin Southampton came along. They were bottom of the league and it seemed that I had a habit of taking on struggling clubs and trying to work miracles. I kept Southampton up and the following season we finished tenth. I went on my holidays that summer and Manchester City came in for me.

They were tough times at City. I had to try and rebuild the squad. They had just escaped relegation the season before. It was very difficult and I think today that you are never given enough time as a manager. The ones who are given time invariably do well. Everybody wants something yesterday.

These days, Alan is found to be offering his opinions on the game on TV and radio. He also does after-dinner speaking and sports forums, captivating audiences eager to find what makes this great hero tick. He still goes back to Goodison from time to time to watch his beloved club in action.

It is a mystery as to why, so far, his management career has not been as successful as it probably should have been, especially with the standards that Alan has lived by in all his football-playing career. When asked if he had ever harboured thoughts about applying and then managing the club where he had his greatest football times, he said, 'Everybody that has been connected with Everton, been touched by Everton, would do anything for Everton.' That sums up the passion he still feels for the club.

One thing is for certain and that is that when future fans ask their older relatives about players from that golden age in the '60s, Alan Ball will probably be one of the first names that crops up. With his famous mop of red hair and his style of playing the game, Everton fans have been very fortunate to have had such a player to pull on the famous royal blue jersey.

CHAPTER TWO

Sandy Brown

EVERTON PLAYING CAREER: 1963–1971
GAMES PLAYED: 256
GOALS SCORED: 54

Some players will always be regarded with affection by Evertonians. Sandy Brown is part of Everton folklore. All because of a goal scored in a derby match. Against Everton! Yet there was more to Sandy than met the eye. In September 1963 Sandy was brought to Goodison by that ever-shrewd judge of players, Harry Catterick. Signed from Partick Thistle for £38,000, this utility player gave his all for the club. He was a real all-round action man. Hard but fair. Ask him to play out of position and he would just get on with it. He even ended up in goal a few times. And to think he could have actually scored *that* goal wearing a red shirt instead of the blue he wore for nearly eight years.

I was at a Scotland versus Ireland game and was told to get ready to travel to Liverpool. I didn't know who I was going to see. At the time, Liverpool were interested in signing me before Everton came in. Of the two, I wanted to join Everton because they had won the Championship the previous season and I thought I could be a winner with them. But apparently Liverpool were ready to make an offer of a swap deal with Geoff Strong plus cash, but Roger Byrne broke his arm at Wembley and the deal was off. So when I was told to travel to Liverpool, I thought I was going to Anfield. It didn't click that I was going to Goodison at all. There was even confusion about the price that Everton were to pay. I was told it was £38,000, but it was much less. Anyway, I was just happy to sign for Everton because they were *the* team and the money was good too. Twenty-five pounds a week. I was delighted. It was more than a lot of my friends were on at the time.

To say that Sandy was impressed with the facilities would be an understatement.

> What I had been used to was nothing more than a dog track in those days when they had evening races at Partick. I had never seen a ground like Goodison before. The place was huge and kind of scary. I could understand the opposition not particularly wanting to play there. The players made me feel at home straightaway. In those days Everton were very much like a family club. Everyone helped me settle in including the chairman, the late Sir John Moores. Every so often we would go and play golf up at St Annes near where he lived and afterwards go back to his home for something to eat and drink.

Sandy settled in well at Goodison. Playing on either side of the back four in an exciting team, Sandy became known as a tough but fair tackler who could, on a number of occasions, push into midfield. Not renowned for his goalscoring talents, Sandy treasured every one. He was not interested in who scored as long as the team won. However, Sandy admits that going in goal usually brought him into friendly conflict with Gordon West. You see, whenever Gordon had to leave the pitch, Sandy was the nominated goalkeeper, a position he did not relish. This was because if Sandy made a mistake, Gordon would let him have an earful for the rest of the week.

> I remember being in goal on a few occasions. Woe betide me if I got it wrong. Gordon would give me a hard time. I didn't mind really. I remember being up at Newcastle and Gordon had been sent off. They had got a penalty and I went in goal. Of course the first thing I did was pick the ball out of the net. The amount of stick I got on the coach coming home off Gordon was really bad. He kept going on about how many times he had told me to keep an eye on the ball. Trouble was I kept an eye on it as it went into the net. I'd like to think that the fans were a bit more forgiving. Even when we were training, Gordon was the mickey-taker. At least he made training as light-hearted as possible. Mind you there were a lot of big personalities at the club. One person I did feel sorry for was Tony Kay. He got caught up in a major scandal and that virtually finished his career. He was a superb talent and a really nice bloke.

The one match that Sandy remembers most is one that he did not play in – the FA Cup final in 1966.

Just being there that day will be something I'll never forget. I remember at half-time thinking that we had probably lost this one. I sat there on the bench with my head in my hands. I was thinking 'I wish I could help the lads', but I accepted that I would not be getting onto the pitch. Harry had decided on the team and that was that. Then we got back into it followed by Derek Temple's goal. The whole end where the supporters were erupted. What a noise! How could anyone forget that day. The trouble was I ended up playing in three semi-finals and never played at Wembley. To tell you how great the club were in looking after the players, we each were given fifty pounds by Sir John Moores after the game as the bonus.

By now both Merseyside clubs were winning major domestic trophies. The players from both teams used to mix socially as well.

Quite often a few of us would challenge some of the Reds to rounds of golf. There would be St John, Ron Yeats and a few others. They were not bad players but I'd be the one who wanted to beat them every time. After a round we'd end up in the pub and just talk football. We could only go to the pub before Wednesday because we were not allowed to drink alcohol after Wednesday, before a match. It was one of Harry's rules. Of course Bill Shankly approved of it as well. After all both Harry and Bill were the two top managers at the time. I'm sure they must have swapped notes.

Everton went on building a team that would eventually win the league. In the 1967–68 season Sandy was often used as a substitute. Ray Wilson had established himself as the left-back and Tommy Wright as the right-back. In this position Sandy was able to see how some of the younger players were coming through the ranks.

Joe Royle had just broken into the team. The fans were not happy because he had replaced Alex [Young], and that was a hard act to follow, but Joe handled it all very well. Another one was Alan Whittle. He was very talented and he proved valuable in the last part of the Championship battle of the 1969–70 season.

All good things come to an end and Sandy left the club in 1971 to join Shrewsbury Town. It was a wrench to leave the club that for him had played a very important part in his life.

It broke my heart to have to leave. But these things happen. You always think that it can go on forever. I joined Shrewsbury and stayed there for about a season and then I went to Southport in 1972. That was great as I played in a successful side. We won the Fourth Division Championship that season and I was glad to be part of it all.

Not long after that season Sandy retired from playing. He did harbour ambitions towards the coaching side of the game but they never materialised. He worked in a slipper factory for a while, and then he finished his working life in a biscuit factory in Blackpool, where he still lives today. Last September Sandy suffered a stroke but it still didn't stop him making an appearance at his favourite 'home', Goodison Park, in April 1997. He was invited to step back onto the pitch to make a presentation at half-time to a fan who had won the club's lottery. Of course the game the officials wanted Sandy to be present for was a derby match. It certainly brought back the memories.

> What a night that was! I was with Brian Labone and Dave Hickson. Just before we walked up the steps, my heart started to thump away and my stomach was turning. I was just like a kid again. The reception I got from the fans was terrific. Just a sea of faces and a wall of sound. Looking around the place I noticed it hadn't changed all that much except it was a bit bigger with that new stand at the Park End.

In our interview with Sandy for this book, we could not let *that* goal go unmentioned. For those of you readers who were not there at the derby that day in December 1969, Sandy scored with an incredible flying 'header'. Only trouble was . . . it was for Liverpool.

> I should get royalties every time it's mentioned. I don't know why I went for it. There didn't seem to be any danger. It must have been a rush of blood to the head or something. After it went in, I think I was more worried about the stick I was going to get from Gordon rather than the fans. Mind you it was a great header.

In talking to Sandy, you know that he still has a great affection for Everton. He was a superb team player. As long as the team did well Sandy was happy. And to think he could have ended up playing in a red shirt rather than a blue one.

CHAPTER THREE

Bobby Collins

EVERTON PLAYING CAREER: 1958–1962
GAMES PLAYED: 147
GOALS SCORED: 48

There have been few players in the history of the club who can claim to have made every inch of his height and every ounce of weight count for more than Bobby Collins. He may only have stood 5 ft 4 in., but this dynamic Glaswegian was an inspirational midfield general, dominating games with his force of character, will to win, sheer grandeur and fire – and no little skill into the bargain.

Affectionately dubbed the 'Pocket Napoleon', Collins was perpetual motion, as he chased every lost cause down, never shirked a bone-crunching tackle and made a nuisance of himself, as he tried to lift the Blues from the doldrums of the '50s towards a brighter future.

Collins actually signed for Everton in September 1958 for a fee of £23,500. But Everton could easily have saved themselves this outlay had Collins joined the club in 1947 after he'd had trials at Goodison. But a certain degree of homesickness hit the teenaged Collins, and he elected to go back home to Glasgow and throw in his lot with Celtic.

So successful was Collins that he gained his first of 31 Scottish caps before his 20th birthday in 1950, and he caught the eye of several top English clubs before he was finally persuaded to sign on the line for the Blues. This was one of Ian Buchan's last acts as manager, before giving way to Johnny Carey. But if the signing was shrewd, then Buchan's decision to play Collins as a striker puzzled football lovers everywhere.

Collins had proved to be something of a prolific goalscorer in Scotland towards the end of his time at Celtic, so Buchan believed that he would get the best out of him up front. Collins, needless to say, wasn't at all happy with the position, and quickly persuaded Carey to push him back into midfield.

> I could only play one way, and that was the way that came naturally to me. There was simply no other way. But overall I had marvellous times at Everton. I had no problems adapting to the English game after coming down from Glasgow. I just got on with it. Mind you, I'm still not sure why I ended up going there. After all, when I joined the club they'd just lost six games in a row or something!

Made captain by Carey, Collins proved to be a vital well-spring of influence for the club as the manager struggled to get things moving. And in his first two full seasons at the club, Collins netted an astonishing 31 goals, which would have been a decent return for a striker in a good side, but for a midfield man in a struggling outfit it was phenomenal.

By the time that Harry Catterick arrived on the scene, Collins was seen as arguably the most important player at the club. As Brian Labone recalls:

> Bobby was just brilliant. People who were lucky enough to see him play will have great memories of just how great he was. And if you never saw him, then you missed something very special. He is one of the best players ever to play for the club, no question.

However, Catterick decided that at 31 years of age, Collins was too old to figure in his long-term strategy for the club, and he decided to let him go. Dennis Stevens came in from Bolton to replace him, and after a brief flirtation on the right wing, he was sold to Leeds.

> I suppose Harry looked at the fee he got for me [£30,000] as being good business. He made a profit on me in the transfer market, and at my age probably felt that I was on the way out. Harry was like that: very aware of the business side of things. Of course, I was disappointed to leave, but once the manager makes his mind up there's nothing a player can do but accept the decision and get on with his career. And if Harry hadn't put me up for sale, I'd never have got the chance to play for Leeds!

Collins's tenure at Leeds gave the lie to those who thought that his career was on the slide. He led Leeds to the second division championship in 1963–64, took them to their first FA Cup final a year later (they lost 2–1 to

Liverpool after extra time) and was voted Footballer of the Year in 1965, even earning a recall to the Scotland team that same year.

Strangely, Collins might have been doing all of this across Stanley Park. On the very day that he agreed to drop down a division and join Leeds, Bill Shankly made a bid to bring him to Anfield. He tried again the following season, but both attempts failed. How galling would it have been for every True Blue to watch Collins in a red shirt?!

Collins carried on playing until he was 42, giving his all in the cause of Bury, Morton, Ringwood (in Australia) and Oldham, before hanging up his boots in 1973. But it was inevitable that Collins would maintain his strong links with the game.

> I had a brief spell as a coach at Oldham, which gave me some useful experience. Then I moved on to Huddersfield for my first job in management, but that didn't turn out so good. And I didn't last very long.

In fact, after leaving Huddersfield in 1974, Collins had to wait until 1977 to get another crack in the management game, this time on Humberside at Hull City.

> Again, that didn't turn out so good for me and I didn't last long there either. By then, Norman Hunter, my old Leeds team-mate, had taken over as manager of Barnsley, and he brought me in as youth-team coach. Norman had four great years there, but what did he get for his pains? The sack. And I was asked to take over in 1984. In my first season at Oakwell, we finished sixth in the league and reached the last eight of the FA Cup. And would you know it, I was actually fired myself! It was unbelievable and quite unreal. Most clubs would have been satisfied with that for a first season, but not Barnsley. So, I followed Norman out of the door very quickly!

Now retired ('I don't do anything more strenuous than sign the odd autograph here and there!'), Collins still makes occasional visits back to Goodison, especially when swords are crossed between Everton and Leeds. But what does he think of modern-day football?

> There's no doubt that they're very fit indeed. They can all run and have amazing stamina. But honestly, how many really great footballers are there in the game today as compared to the number around when I was playing? But I still enjoy watching games.

As for his time at Everton, Collins has nothing but fond memories. No medals, but lots of happy times . . .

They were marvellous times at Goodison. For me, things went really well, and I was obviously delighted to have the chance of playing with such players as Dave Hickson. He was such a smashing player and a great header of the ball for a man his size! No, I am really pleased to have had the chance to play for Everton. I will always have a fond feeling towards the club.

CHAPTER FOUR

Martin Dobson

EVERTON PLAYING CAREER: 1974–1979
GAMES PLAYED: 230
GOALS SCORED: 40

In another era, another time, Martin Dobson would have been hailed as the world-class midfield star who inspired Everton to glory. A cultured, stylish visionary, Dobson was the complete midfield maestro, at home bustling, hustling and tackling, as well as striking the ball smoothly over considerable yardage to a grateful team-mate. He also had an underrated, explosive shot capable of reaching blistering velocity, as Liverpool witnessed in 1976 when Dobson rasped in a 40-yard goal past Ray Clemence at Anfield. He played in an Everton team that never quite scaled the heights. A team full of talent, yet one that lived in the lengthy shadow cast by their deadly rivals at Anfield.

Dobson started his career, as did many of the game's finest players in the '60s and '70s, with unfashionable Burnley, a club who survived through developing players via an incomparable youth system and then selling them on to bigger clubs. Dobson was the beneficiary/victim of this system when he joined the Blues in August 1974.

The transfer came as a complete surprise, I must admit. There was something in the press over the weekend – after we'd played Ipswich – about Everton's interest in me, but I didn't believe that I would be the next one out of the club. Now, I knew that Burnley were going to have to sell a player to help finance a new stand they were planning on building – that was the way at Turf Moor. And it really was going to come down to either me or Welsh winger Leighton James being let go. But I thought that I was safe for the time being. After all, I was club captain, playing really well and felt that I was part of the fixtures and fittings at the club. In fact, I thought that I would be at the club for ever.

Then, after we trained on the Monday following the Ipswich match, the assistant manager of Burnley, Joe Brown, had a word with me and explained that the club had agreed a huge fee [£300,000] with Everton for my services. He told me that it was my decision as to whether or not I wanted to go and talk to Everton, but I really felt that I was being pushed into leaving, and was being left with virtually no choice in the matter. The deal had already been done.

These days, with every player having their own agent, things might have been different. I'd have had time to think over things, to discuss them with someone else working on my behalf and to have made a reasoned, careful decision as to whether it was in my best interests to leave Burnley for Everton. But I didn't have any advisors. I was on my own. And within 24 hours I'd signed for Everton.

Now, to be honest, I don't regret making the move. But what I did resent at the time was that Burnley's manager, Jimmy Adamson, never spoke to me about why the club were selling me. I really would have liked a chance to sit down with him and talk things through, just to understand his thinking. But I never got the opportunity. It was all very disappointing to me.

Although Dobson was to go on and make a major name for himself at Everton, at first things were difficult, not least because he didn't see eye-to-eye with manager Billy Bingham on the way football should be played.

I was spoilt a little at Burnley. We concentrated on the positive side of the game, we loved expressing ourselves on the pitch. We were encouraged to attack and to take a really adventurous line. But Billy Bingham, well, I found him to be very defensively minded. He seemed to want to get everyone behind the ball and just defend all the time. Sure, we would win 1–0, but it was so boring, for the players and fans alike.

Typical of that era was my début, against Arsenal. We did win 2–1, but it was just dull. There was very little for anyone to get excited about.

Everything changed, says Dobson, with the arrival in early 1977 of Gordon Lee to replace the sacked Bingham.

Things started to pick up as soon as Gordon arrived. The years from 1977 until I left in '79 were terrific. We played some great football, we entertained and we all enjoyed what we were doing. I forged a really great partnership down the left with winger Dave Thomas and full-back Mike Pejic. We were known collectively as the Bermuda Triangle, because players would disappear into this area of the field where we operated, and they wouldn't be seen again! Both on the pitch and off it, the three of us got on really well. We shared a lot of interests and became great friends, which helped our understanding when playing for the club. I think it helps when people genuinely like playing with each other – and that was certainly the case with the three of us.

When I first went to Everton, though, I roomed with George Telfer, who was a really nice guy. George and I got on very well and we became good friends. But Dave Thomas, Mike Pejic and I were really very tight.

Sadly, those years were not capped by silverware or other honours. As Dobson points out, Everton were very much the 'nearly' club at the time, always on the verge of achieving something special, but never able to break through.

Liverpool were the dominant force in England and Europe at the time, which made life so difficult for all of us. If you look at our record on its own, it was quite good; we were so close, so often, to making that all-important breakthrough and winning a trophy. But because it was Liverpool who regularly swept the board, we were regarded as a failure. But all of us who played in that team really felt that if only we could have won just one cup, then it could have transformed everything. Yet, we never got a lucky break.

Like most players of the era, Dobson retains enormous affection and respect for Gordon Lee.

He was straight, honest and such a football enthusiast. He was desperate for us to succeed and just loved the game. His belief rubbed off on all of the players and gave us the confidence to go out and play some great stuff. Of course, he was a little naïve. Gordon once said that he didn't feel there was anything he could learn from European football – and remember, this was at a time when Holland were dominating the world with their total football approach. When players like Cruyff and Neeskens were setting new standards. Also, when West Germany were virtually unbeatable. So, Gordon's comments didn't stand him in good stead as far as the outside world was concerned. It made him look rather stupid, which was a real shame.

Of course, I'm not suggesting that Gordon got on with everyone at the club. One player who certainly did not see eye-to-eye with him was Duncan McKenzie, but then Duncan was very much his own man. He was an entertainer who played to the crowds. He would like nothing better than taking on three or four defenders and trying to get past them, even if someone was better placed. I lost count of the number of times Dunc would do something that looked absolutely brilliant, but then lost the ball. The fans loved him for it, but we'd all be calling him a pillock under our breath. So, it was no wonder he could never get used to Gordon.

But there's no doubt that under Gordon Lee, Everton developed a real style and flair. Like I said, if only we could have won something . . .

Perhaps Everton never came nearer winning a major honour under Lee than in 1977 when the team reached the FA Cup semi-final, facing the dreaded old enemy, Liverpool, at Maine Road. The game will always be remembered by Evertonians for arguably the most controversial and talked-about refereeing decision in the club's history, as Dobson explained.

The game was poised at 2–2, when our substitute Bryan Hamilton put the ball into the net. Everyone thought it was the winner – including the Liverpool players. But then the ref, Clive Thomas, disallowed it. Why? He said it was for an 'infringement', but would not elaborate – still hasn't. It couldn't have been for offside, because the linesman kept his flag down. Maybe Thomas thought Bryan had handled the ball, but there was not even a murmur of protest from the Liverpool players – and that tells you something! No, it remains a mystery, and one which snatched away what would have been a deserving victory for us.

It must have been even worse for poor old Bryan, because a couple of years earlier something similar had happened to him when he was at Ipswich. Clive Thomas had disallowed a 'goal' for reasons which were never fully explained or revealed. God, how Bryan must have hated the sight of Clive Thomas!

I was actually lucky to have started the semi-final at all. I was carrying a groin strain from the week before, and it was touch and go right up to the kick-off whether I would be fit enough to take my place in the line-up. I had to have an injection from the Manchester City club doctor in order to make sure that I could get on the pitch. But, to be honest, I really struggled in the first 45 minutes and had to come off at half-time, which let on Bryan!

I was sitting close to Gordon when that third goal was ruled out, and to say he was bitterly disappointed was an understatement! He was desperately upset, as we all were. To have been so close to an FA Cup final, and to have it cruelly snatched away from us like that was just awful – especially because it was against Liverpool. Maybe we wouldn't have beaten Man United in the final, who can say? But at least we'd have given the fans a day out at Wembley, which they deserved for the way they stuck by us in those times.

Everton lost the replay, again at Maine Road. And once more Dobson had to have a pain-killing injection before the match.

On a brighter note, 'Dobbo' recalls a game the following season against Chelsea, when he scored twice to bring the Blues back from 2–1 behind at Goodison.

It was Duncan McKenzie's homecoming as it were, his first game at Goodison after his switch to Chelsea. And the atmosphere was great. Dunc scored to give Chelsea the lead, but then I struck with two headers from Dave Thomas crosses. It was a game that really sticks in my mind. In a way, the result was the best possible for the fans. Duncan had scored, but we'd won.

But Dobson's period at Goodison was ultimately one of frustration. So near, yet so far. He didn't even manage to add more than one cap to his poor collection of just five England caps, four of which came during his time at Burnley. Still, he was quite prepared to see out his playing career with the Goodison club – that is, if the powers-that-be could be persuaded to give him a lengthy contract in 1979.

I wanted a three-year deal. The club didn't agree to giving me such a long contract at my age [Dobson was 31]. They only offered me two years more. So I made the decision to leave. Look, I enjoyed my time at Goodison. I have really fond memories, but I just felt that if they couldn't give me a three-year deal, then I wasn't going to hang around.

Dobson made the rather surprising choice of returning to Burnley for a fee of £100,000, a move he now regards as perhaps being the wrong one to have made. 'Leeds were interested in me, as were Nantes in France. But I suppose the chance to go back home swung it for me. But things just didn't quite work out the way I hoped. The first season back, we were relegated!'

In 1984, Dobson decided it was time to try to plunge into the murky waters of management. He accepted the post of player-manager at lowly Bury, where he really learnt about life at the bottom of the ladder.

We had very little money to speak of, so I had to rely on the club's youth system and also picking up players on free transfers. But I enjoyed some success at the club and even brought in a few players who went on to achieve something in the game.

For instance, I got a youngster called Andy Hill from Manchester United, and he went on to play for Manchester City and do quite well for himself. I even made him captain of the club at one point. Then there was Jamie Hoyland, who also went on to better things.

But my biggest success came with a full-back called Lee Dixon. I knew him from my time at Burnley and knew he had a special talent. So I got him to Bury and he was absolutely brilliant. But Lee wanted the security of a contract and we couldn't give him one. At this time, Mick Mills was manager at Stoke, and he had Lee watched a few times, and eventually came in for him. I told our board that we should hold out for a £100,000 fee because I knew he was worth every penny. But Stoke offered far less, which disappointed me. Eventually, the whole matter went before a tribunal and we got a fee of £40,000, which was peanuts compared to his real worth. What's more, we didn't even get a percentage of any future transfer, which was something I'm sure would be built into a similar deal now.

Gordon Taylor, from the PFA, actually sat on the tribunal panel. And two or three months later, he called and admitted to me that they had underestimated Lee's value. The problem was nobody sitting on the tribunal had ever seen him play, so they couldn't really judge for themselves. It was honest of Gordon to make that admission, but it was far too late to do anything about the decision. Bury just lost out.

When Arsenal started to show an interest in Lee, their manager at the time, George Graham, actually phoned up and asked my opinion on the player. I told him that Lee was capable of playing at the very highest levels. And, whilst I don't think I swayed George one way or the other, I like to think I played a small role in helping Lee on his way in a career where he's earned a lot of honours, including playing for England.

Dobson finally left Bury in 1989, under slightly difficult conditions. 'It was all a bit messy really. I was given a new contract, but things just were not working out as I hoped, and I ended up leaving the club.'
Without an immediate employer, Dobson spent a short period out of the game, before Bristol Rovers hired him as their new manager in 1991.

They were in the old second division when I joined. I was there for just three months before leaving, but that was my fault entirely. We got off to a bad start, and after three months I called a meeting with the chairman to put forward proposals for the team. I told him exactly how I wanted things done. He refused, and so I quit. To be honest, I acted very naïvely, and probably didn't really give the job a chance, but you learn from your mistakes.

Dobson turned to coaching at schools, as well as helping out his wife in her business ('I did some book-keeping for her'). And, in 1992, he even had a spell out in Cyprus, working for Apop FC. But it was the schools' side that was building up nicely – and would have continued to do so, were it not for Bolton.

The year the club were relegated from the premiership [1995–96], Bolton's manager Colin Todd offered me the job of youth development officer. He outlined his long-term goals and ambitions and said that he wanted me on board to help set up a centre of excellence, which appealed to me enormously.

So that's where I am at the moment. Bolton are upwardly mobile, we've learnt from our mistakes in 1995–96 and the youth side of things is getting strong support from everyone at the club. I think we're going places. This is an exciting place to be, what with the new ground and the fresh challenge of building something that can take Bolton on to winning things.

But wherever he might be employed, Dobson retains a special place for Everton.

Oh yes, you can't play for a club like Everton for as long as I did without getting a real sense of affection for the place, for the fans and for the people you played with. Even in the worst of times we would still get crowds of about 40,000 at Goodison. And it was a fantastic stadium to play in. As I said before, I loved my time there with Gordon Lee enormously. I know I left before he did, but I still believe – as we all do from that period – that had we won just one trophy, then the floodgates would have opened, and who knows what the club might have gone on to achieve. But football isn't about what might have been. You have to deal in realities, and the truth is we didn't win anything.

CHAPTER FIVE

Brian Harris

EVERTON PLAYING CAREER: 1954–1966
GAMES PLAYED: 358
GOALS SCORED: 29

Were it not for an administrative cock-up (to use the technical term), Brian Harris could well have ended up wearing the red of Liverpool rather than the blue of Everton – and history might have been changed radically.

I have to admit that I was actually a Liverpool fan as a lad. My father used to take me along regularly to Anfield, and I'd stand in the boys' pen up on the Kop. Anyway, I played for my local schoolboys' team in Port Sunlight on the right wing, and I was spotted by a scout from Liverpool, who came round to see me and my parents. He offered me a trial at the club, which was fine by me. Two weeks later, I received a letter from Liverpool inviting me along to take part in a match at their training ground, Mellwood. But the time on the letter was 2.45 p.m. I thought, 'They only want me to come along and play for a half. I'm not having that!' I didn't think that I could really show them what I was all about in 45 minutes. So, I didn't bother turning up. It just seemed to me that either I was allowed to play for the whole game, or it wasn't worth the effort.

Then an Everton scout saw me in action for Port Sunlight, and again asked me to go along for a trial. They wanted me to play in a testimonial match at Chester for 45 minutes, which again wasn't ideal, but I thought that I'd better not pass up this opportunity because another one may not come along. So, I went down to the game, ended up playing for the whole 90 minutes and scored twice. We won 5–1 that day.

But there is a sting to the story. The Liverpool scout who first spotted me, when he found out that I hadn't turned up, rang up to ask me what happened. I explained that the letter had said 2.45 on it and that they obviously weren't that keen, and he just said, 'Oh, that was a typing error, it should have said 12.45!' So, but for that typing mistake, I might have ended up at Anfield and not Goodison!

Fortunately for the Goodison club, by the time Liverpool realised the typing error had occurred, Harris had, in January 1954, already signed up for Everton. When he arrived at the club, Harris was somewhat in awe of the place and the personalities.

Cliff Britton was the manager when I joined. And I would sit in team talks, just listening to what he had to say, not daring to open my mouth and say a word. So I really didn't get to know him that well. But he did give me my début and like most players I'll never forget that day. It was against Burnley at Turf Moor in late 1955. Jimmy Harris and I both made our débuts in that game on either wing. We won 1–0, and the late Harry Potts scored the winner for us. Strange thing about Harry, he of course went on to manage Burnley quite successfully in the '60s.

And Harris also has good cause to remember his first trip to London with the club.

Yes, I certainly recall that one. In those days, we used to travel down by train from Lime Street. We didn't have the luxury coaches used by clubs these days. Anyway, not knowing about protocol, I turned up at the station and got in the first carriage I saw with empty seats – except that there were a few of the major names from the team at the time already in there, people like Peter Farrell who I really looked up to. I shouldn't have been there at all. But by the time I'd realised my error, the train had pulled out of the station. It was too late! So, I sat there throughout the journey being ignored, feeling very uncomfortable, not daring to say a word in front of these top players. It was an awful trip!

Johnny Carey was manager of the club when Harris broke into the first team on a regular basis and unlike many others, Brian doesn't exactly have fond memories of the ebullient, extrovert Irishman.

No, I do not. He favoured the Irish contingent at the club and the two of us did not get on at all. I got a lot of bollockings from him because he wanted me to pass the ball more often. We were always arguing and he left me out of the side on a number of occasions. The day he was fired, I was out playing golf. And let's just say that when the news came through, I had a few bevvies and literally had to be carried home!

By the time Harry Catterick arrived as Carey's replacement in 1961, Harris had already been switched from the right wing to become a left-half (as the position was known in those days), so whatever else Carey may or may not have done to further Harris's career and position at the club, this stroke certainly did bring out hitherto unknown qualities in the player.

Like I said, I played on the right wing when I first broke into the team, but then I got an injury and lost my place, ending up back in the reserves, which was demoralising. But then one day Jimmy Tansey, who was the left-half at the time, got injured, and for some reason I was asked to take his place. God knows why I was asked. But I did really well and that's where I ended up sticking for the rest of my career.

Harris started out as a regular in the 1962–63 championship season, but was displaced by Tony Kay, when that classy player arrived from Sheffield Wednesday with a growing reputation and stature.

The day Tony arrived was a very strange one for me. After training, I'd gone into Liverpool city centre with Gordon West, Brian Labone and Jimmy Gabriel to one of the coffee shops, or somewhere. Now, there were rumours going round at the time that Tony was about to sign, so I'd gone in to see Harry that very morning to find out what was going on. After all, it was my position that was in jeopardy and I wanted to find out where I stood. Harry totally denied that Everton were even talking to Tony and convinced me that the whole story was media rubbish. So I went away believing that my position was safe in the team.

Anyway, as I said, I was out in town that very afternoon when the *Liverpool Echo* announced that Everton had actually just signed Tony Kay! I was stunned, to say the least. Harry had clearly known when I'd spoken to him that morning what was about to happen and couldn't even tell me. I know he had a reputation for being secretive about incoming transfers, not liking word to get out before the deal was done, but I feel he could at least have given me a hint, or at least not been so strong in his denial. I felt that I'd been bullshitted by my own manager, and I was not very pleased – to put it mildly!

An angry Harris understandably put in a transfer request. But nothing actually happened.

> Oh, after that whole affair I wanted away. I felt that I'd been treated very badly and just couldn't carry on at the club – and who can blame me? It was time to leave. I put in a transfer request, which was accepted by the manager and the board of directors, but nothing much happened. Manchester City were said to be interested, but they didn't follow through with a firm offer, so I stayed put. And not long after that I actually got back into the first team, at left-back.

But fate was to take a hand in Harris's rollercoaster career. Having resigned himself to being an Everton also-ran, he was plunged straight back into the blue spotlight when Kay was banned from football for his part in the infamous 1960s' match-fixing scandal, which happened while he was still at Hillsborough, but only took effect when he'd joined Everton.

Back in the team, albeit under such strange circumstances, Harris never looked back, making the left-half berth his own and being a crucial part of the 1966 FA Cup-winning team.

> That was such a brilliant day for all of us. Playing at Wembley on such an occasion is every player's dream. And to have it come true was a real highlight of my career. So many great players never got the chance to play in a cup final. So, for me, it was a real pinnacle. And what a game, eh? We were the clear favourites to win the Cup, but we struggled to get our rhythm going. To be honest, we didn't do ourselves or our fans justice on the day, and it was only when we went two goals down that we started to perform.
>
> Did we think that we'd lost the game at 2–0? I don't think we actually had any time to think properly. After their second goal, we got one back right away thanks to Mike Trebilcock, so we were back in the hunt. Had we not scored so soon after Wednesday got their second, we would probably have lost it, but as things turned out . . . well, we did it!

The match will always be remembered for the Everton fan who ran onto the pitch after Trebilcock got his – and the team's – second goal to bring the scores level at 2–2. He ran across the pitch, took off his jacket to avoid one policeman's desperate lunge, and was eventually rugby-tackled by another, crashing to the ground only yards from the Everton goal. Harris recalls the fan now with a mild chuckle. 'Yeah, it was Eddy Cavanagh. He must have been the first hooligan to get on TV. I saw him not so long ago. He's an Everton legend in his own right – and I think he's got something like 17 kids!'

During this era as well, Harris also came very close to earning a well-deserved cap for England.

It was back in our championship season, 1962–63. Alf Ramsey called me to the squad, but unfortunately I had to withdraw because of injury. And I was never selected again. In those days, you didn't get too many chances to play for England, and if you didn't grab an opportunity with both hands, you got forgotten. I suppose that's what happened to me.

All of which leaves Harris as one of the best uncapped players in the history of the club. In fact, of the 1966 Toffee heroes, only the dependable left-half and the goalscoring sensation Mike Trebilcock were destined never to be selected for their country. And as Trebilcock disappeared from Everton just as quickly as he appeared, perhaps it's only Harris who can really be regarded as unlucky not to win a full cap.

And that heady FA Cup day at Wembley effectively proved to be Harris's swan song for Everton. He was soon on his way out.

I picked up a thigh injury on a pre-season tour of Ireland at the beginning of the next season, which sidelined me for two months. By the time I was fit again, things had changed. Alan Ball had arrived from Blackpool and made a huge impact, and Harry was drastically rebuilding the side. I was 31 years old, and he probably felt I had little future at the club. So he let me go. I was sad to leave because I had so many memories, but it was better for me to get a regular slot in a lower division side than just to languish in Everton's reserves.

Harris dropped down a division, moving to Cardiff City. But he was about to experience one of the greatest footballing experiences of his life. Unfancied, unheralded, Cardiff reached the European Cup Winners' Cup semi-finals in 1968, (Harris's second season there), getting to within a whisker of the final itself. Only a late goal from SV Hamburg's legendary Uwe Seeler at Ninian Park put paid to the Welsh club's glorious progress.

How ironic that Everton, one of the giants of the British game, should continue to underachieve in Europe right through until the mid-'80s, whilst the minnows of Cardiff came so close to Euro-glory.

At Cardiff I was the senior player and everyone else looked up to me, which was a bit strange at first. But I really enjoyed my time there. It was a very different set-up from Everton. The club were obviously not as big, but that made the success we had even more satisfying, because it was so unexpected.

The European run in '68 was just like a dream. It was incredible. I remember in one of the earlier rounds we played a Russian team. Their captain didn't speak any English and I, of course, don't speak Russian, which made communication virtually impossible. Before the first game, we met in the ref's dressing-room and this Russian kept making strange hand gestures, which looked to me like he was being threatening. So anyway I ignored him. But he did the same before the second leg, which really got on my nerves. I thought he wanted to pick a fight with me. But somebody told me afterwards that all this poor chap was trying to ask was whether I wanted to go out with him for a drink. Talk about misunderstanding. I could have escalated the cold war there and then!

Reaching the semi-finals of a major European competition with any team would been special, but with a team like Cardiff it was really quite something. Who knows what would have happened had we actually made it to the final, but to be that close meant an awful lot in the way that people looked at Welsh football.

Harris eventually left Cardiff but stayed put in Wales, securing a managerial post at Newport County – his first and last attempt in that role.

The first season I had at Newport, things went really well. In fact, I got them to within a whisker of promotion. But that was the end of the good times there. In the end I quit because I had a row with the chairman, Cyril Rogers, over a transfer. It was really the last straw and left a bitter taste in my mouth. Let's just say I wasn't being allowed to develop the team as I wanted, so I had to leave.

That wasn't the total end of Harris's involvement with football, but he was never again to take a full-time position.

I'd just had enough of the game at that point I suppose. If Everton had come in for me and offered me a coaching job I might have taken it, but as it was I drifted into the insurance game for a while. I did all right at it, but it was very different after years in football.

Mind you, I did still keep my hand in with the game to a certain extent. I'd met a guy called Bobby Ferguson during my time at Cardiff and we kept in touch after I left the club. Bobby ended up as Bobby Robson's number two at Ipswich during their great days in the late '70s and he asked me to do some scouting for them. That was something I truly enjoyed – until I went back to Goodison for a game.

Now, having been at the club for so many years, I thought I'd go early to see old friends and savour the atmosphere once more. But when my wife and I tried to get into one of the lounges at Everton, the 300 Club or something like that, the jobsworth on the door wouldn't let us in! I wasn't a member, you see. It didn't matter that I'd spent more than 12 years at the club. That counted for nothing as far as this person was concerned. It was embarrassing! Fortunately, I bumped into someone working at the club whom I knew from my playing days, and they put me and my wife into the players' lounge, where we just sat on our own until kick-off time! The whole thing left me feeling rather sad about the way the club seemed to be treating former player.

Fortunately, that hasn't put Harris off returning to his old stamping ground – and during Joe Royle's tenure as Goodison manager he did just that, receiving a much warmer reception.

Towards the end of my playing days, I used to look after Joe when he was a teenager just breaking into the team. And when he came in as manager, Joe was kind enough to invite me back. I must admit it was a great ego trip walking down the road to the ground and being recognised after all these years. It made me feel really good.

These days, Harris, based in Leeds, works in promotions with various local papers in the north of England.

What happened was that a few years ago I played golf with a guy who just happened to be the director of the *Yorkshire Evening Post*. I love playing golf these days, it's one of my favourite pastimes. Anyway, I was discussing some ideas for helping to promote the paper. One thing led to another, and here I am working with a number of papers. My wife and two sons are also involved in the business.

And Brian even finds time to play football occasionally. 'Well, I play in charity games every so often. The last one I appeared in, I ended up in goal. And I can tell you I am no Gordon West! Still, it was fun.'

Brian Harris was one of the unsung heroes of a truly golden period in Everton's history. But while the likes of Alex Young and Ray Wilson gained the headlines in their different ways, Harris, with his unpretentious style, was equally crucial.

CHAPTER SIX

Colin Harvey

EVERTON PLAYING CAREER: 1962–1974
GAMES PLAYED: 384
GOALS SCORED: 24
EVERTON MANAGERIAL CAREER: 1987–1990

Kendall, Ball and Harvey. Even now, nearly 30 years after they last played together in the royal blue of Everton, this trio can still send shivers down the proverbial spine, as fans recall their exploits marshalling the midfield area with a combination of skill, vision and enterprise that few have ever matched. Ball's dynamism, perpetual motion and sense of pursuit, and Kendall's sheer power and bravura, rightly made them heroes, with the latter's stock at Goodison increased immeasurably by his first tenure as manager of the club in the mid-'80s. Yet, in many respects, it was the unfussy, unhurried Harvey who provided the glue that held the trio together.

There have been few more elegant, stylish or whole-hearted players in the history of the club than Colin Harvey, an Evertonian in the truest sense of the word. Proud of being able to pull on the blue jersey, the man always gave 100 per cent in the cause of his favourite club, patrolling the midfield area with an economy of effort that belied his commitment to the cause, however forlorn it might seem to others.

Harvey stood on the terraces at Goodison long before he joined the club, watching the likes of Dave Hickson and Bobby Collins, dreaming of the day when he might run out on the pitch.

My dad used to take me along to matches. I would be in the boys' pen, whilst he went in the Gwladys Street End. Afterwards, we'd meet up by the bookshop on the corner of Goodison Road and City Road, which is long gone [it's now a betting shop].

However, it's shocking to recall that Harvey nearly did the unthinkable and join Liverpool as a youngster!

Yes, I did have a trial with them. I even played in a game for them on a Tuesday night. I remember that Ian Callaghan [the celebrated Liverpool winger] was a part-time pro at the club at the time, and he played in the match with me. Anyway, I did well enough for Liverpool to invite me back the following week. Now an uncle of mine actually knew someone at Everton at the time, and word got to the club about me and I was invited down there.

With thoughts of the dreaded reds now banished, Harvey got down to making his mark at his beloved Everton.

I was still at school when I first began playing for the club. What I used to do was play for the school in the morning, and then turn out for Everton's 'C' side in the afternoon. I never told the school about my involvement with Everton, and I didn't tell the club that I was playing for the school!

Leaving school at 16 in 1961, Harvey signed apprentice forms for Everton, and made very rapid progress through the ranks.

I spent a season playing in the 'B' and then 'A' teams, before I got into the reserve side, where I spent a further year. It was all good experience, but I was enjoying it and I never thought that I would be ready to make my first-team début as quickly as I did. And I never dreamt that I would make it in such a major game!

The 'major game' in question was in September 1963. The European Cup first round, second leg, in front of 90,000 fanatical Italians against the mighty Inter Milan at the legendary San Siro Stadium! Talk about a baptism of fire. But Harvey proved that his unquenchable spirit was moulded from asbestos!

Everton had drawn the first leg 0–0, and went out to Italy given little hope by the pundits. Forced to leave behind injured Scottish midfielder Jimmy Gabriel, they took the 18-year-old Harvey on the flight to Milan, but the youngster himself had little reason to believe he was playing.

I thought that I was there just to carry the skips. It wasn't until the afternoon of the game that Harry Catterick told me that I was going to play! To make my début in Everton's first-ever away game in the European Cup was just tremendous, and I really enjoyed it. We ended up losing the game and the tie 1–0, but I didn't have a bad game. I'm not saying that I was brilliant, but I did OK and I certainly didn't feel the pressure. In fact, I took it in my stride to a great extent.

Losing by the odd goal to the team that went on to lift the trophy was no disgrace. However, Harvey had to wait until the 1964–65 season before really establishing himself as a regular.

At first I had a bit of a hard time with some of the big names at the club. I would come in to replace Roy Vernon, or even occasionally Alex Young, and there might have been a little resentment towards me because of this. But once I settled in and became a regular, then they took to me without any problem and looked after me really well.

Unlike most players, Harvey actually enjoyed the rigorous, tough training routines demanded of every player by the club.

Training was a real joy for me. I loved it. Playing games was all about winning. There could be no joy in drawing or losing, but I always looked forward to going out and training. Wilf Dixon [first-team coach at the time] was a hard task-master, but he was also fair, and he didn't come across too many problems as far as I can recall from the players. Actually, I met him again only recently. He must be well into his 70s, but has just taken up golf, and plays three or four times a week. And he looks just great for his age.

Harvey also holds Catterick in awe.

I think he was one of the all-time managerial greats. He was a very underrated manager. People always talk about Bill Shankly, Bill Nicholson, Matt Busby and Don Revie as being the great managers of the '60s and '70s, but Harry's record stands comparison with any of them. He won two championships and the FA Cup during his time as manager, and built teams who played great football. Maybe he never gets due credit because he never really got on with the press, and they never liked him.

As a man, Harry was perhaps a little shy, but he certainly liked to be in control. I always got on well with him. And even when I suffered from injuries, he would always put me straight back in the team as soon as I was fit again.

Catterick's one and only triumph in the FA Cup, of course, came in 1966. And it was Harvey who put the team into the Wembley final.

In the semi-final we beat Manchester United 1–0, and I got one of my rare goals, and with my left foot as well. The year before we made it, I'd gone down to Wembley with a mate to see Liverpool play Leeds in the final. The occasion was just brilliant, and the atmosphere was just unbelievable. I told my mate that one day I would love to play in the Cup final, little thinking that I'd be back within the year as a player!

We got to Wembley without conceding a goal, but our opponents in the final, Sheffield Wednesday, got two within an hour. And for the first 60 minutes they outplayed us. What they did was flood the midfield. Whilst we had Jimmy Gabriel and myself in midfield, with the two wingers – Alex Scott and Derek Temple – out wide, which was normal in those days, they brought their wingers in and effectively had four in midfield. We were outnumbered! But slowly, we got on top of them, and Mike Trebilcock and Derek Temple got the goals that gave us the Cup. I suppose if I had been a Sheffield Wednesday player, I'd have felt disappointed to lose, especially after what happened in the first hour.

The '66 Cup triumph was, in many respects, a watershed for the club, with Catterick revamping the team soon after, replacing some of the older stars with younger, hungrier players . . . and bringing in Ball and Kendall.

Bally arrived as we started to develop a really good footballing side, and when Howard came in as well in 1967, things really began to gel. In 1968, we took it all a stage further, reaching the FA Cup final.

Of course, we won the championship in 1970, but as far as I'm concerned we played better football the season before. The big difference in 1969–70 was that we would win games that the previous year we would draw. We were a bit tougher by then. I'm not saying that we didn't play well in the championship year, because we did. It was just that the level of football was better the previous season.

The 1970 team was packed full of great players all the way through. Sure, the Kendall/Ball/Harvey midfield worked well, but they were not the be all and end all of the team. It helped having so many fabulous players all over the pitch. In 1970 we knew we were the best team in the country, we knew we had the beating of anyone and everyone. But I reckon we'd been the best for three or four years before finally winning the championship. There was always someone in the team who'd do something special.

By the early '70s, though, all the promise of the comparatively young Everton team had gone, along with many of the players. Some look back now and blame Catterick for breaking up a great side that could have scaled even greater heights. But Harvey isn't among them . . .

Sure, by the mid-'70s, Bally had gone, and so had Howard. I was suffering from injuries [first an eye injury and then a hip problem that required a complete replacement]. Lots of players came and went. But that was normal in football – and still is. Success comes in cycles. We'd been competing for honours for a few years, and so the dip in the '70s wasn't unexpected. Only Liverpool seemed to be able to keep their place at the top for a long, unbroken period. Maybe that was the reason why so many people look back on the huge success Liverpool kept getting, and that makes our lack of trophies after 1970 seem even worse. The pressure on Everton just kept on increasing with every honour Liverpool won. But you can't blame Harry for that.

In October 1974, Harvey finally left his beloved Goodison for Sheffield Wednesday, signing for £70,000. But he couldn't recapture his peak form, as injuries continued to plague him. And in December 1975 he finally retired from playing.

I actually had another six months to run on my contract there, but I was frustrated. I could play in games, but couldn't then train for a few days, which I hated so much because I loved training. I just couldn't give 100 per cent any more, and I'm not the sort of person who could live with that. So I walked out of Sheffield Wednesday and gave up the remaining six months' salary I could have drawn just by staying put.

Harvey retired with a championship medal and cup winner's medal, but amazingly only one England cap. And sadly the famed Everton midfield trio never got a chance to work that magic for their country.

I'd been in a few England squads without getting picked. Then in 1969

I went on an England tour to South America, where we played games against Mexico [who would host the World Cup in 1970, of course], Uruguay and Brazil. I never played in any of these, but did get a game against a Mexico XI. But that didn't count as a full international.

Missing out on the World Cup itself, Harvey had to wait until a game against Malta in 1971 for his one and only appearance in an England shirt.

I had been chosen for the England squad again for the 1971 Home Internationals against England, Wales and Northern Ireland after the season finished. But although I got on the bench for two of the matches, I never got on the pitch. So I made my début in Malta, in what was a qualifying game for the 1972 European Nations Cup [now just known as the European Championships].

I was very proud to get that cap. But the pitch we played on . . . it was shale! I'd never seen anything like it, and never did again as a player. It was crazy playing an important international on a pitch like this one. I didn't have a great game, but we did win 1–0, with a goal from Martin Peters.

Harvey believes that then-England boss Sir Alf Ramsey had much in common with his club manager Catterick. He says: 'They were very alike. Both commanded a huge respect from their players, yet also had a suspicion of the press. Maybe Alf was tactically a little shrewder than Harry, but not much.'

Sadly, that was the sum of Harvey's international career. But at least he retired with a cap to his name, and is grateful for having been given one chance.

So, what to do when you're no longer a player? For a time, Harvey amazingly flirted with taking up a career behind the bar. Despite having taken a coaching course at Hillsborough, conducted by Wednesday manager Steve Burtenshaw ('He was a real track-suit manager, and very different to what I was used to at Goodison. He set up a preliminary coaching course which I attended'), Harvey seemed as if he would actually be lost to the game . . . He says: 'I had a couple of uncles who ran pubs. One was in Northwich, and it was a pub where they trained managers, so I worked there for four or five months. It was really hard work, let me tell you.'

But Harvey was saved from pulling pints by the intervention of the Everton manager who had sold him. Billy Bingham rang him up out of the blue and invited the eager Harvey to return to Goodison as youth-team coach. 'It took me all of two seconds to accept the offer! I had a couple of years working with the youth team, and then a few years working with the reserves. And then Howard came back to the club.'

Kendall's return in 1981 as manager, taking over from Gordon Lee, at first seemed destined to fail. But as the remarkable 1983–84 season unfolded, Harvey was promoted to first-team coach, becoming Kendall's right-hand man, and slowly things fitted into place.

People are always asking what was the turning point in that season. What was the catalyst. And there were a few things that happened. Howard bought Andy Gray, who was a larger-than-life character and really galvanised everyone. Trevor Steven, whom we got from Burnley, found his form. And Peter Reid also started to come through.

Actually, when Reidy first arrived at the club [in 1982] he didn't set the place alight, but slowly he discovered his true form, and played a major role. And the team clicked. But there was only one man at the end of the day who was responsible for getting it all to work: Howard. He got everything together, and should take full credit.

The following few years were truly glorious for all Evertonians. And the list of honours snared by the club between 1984 and 1987 still acts like a mantra: two league championships, an FA Cup and a European Cup Winners' Cup. And were it not for the blanket ban on English clubs in Europe after the Heysel Stadium tragedy in 1985, who knows what the team might have achieved?

We were obviously disappointed not to be able to play in the European Cup. That would have been a true test. I know there are a lot of fans and players who are convinced we'd have won the trophy, but you never know in football. Maybe we'd have become European champions, or perhaps we'd have gone out in the first round! But there's no doubt we had a very good team at Everton. I remember one amazing performance early in our 1984–85 championship-winning season, when we thrashed Manchester United 5–0 at Goodison. What a magnificent display we gave that day. And a few days later, we went to Old Trafford and beat them 2–1 in the Milk Cup. United were all out for revenge that night, and they weren't a bad side, so for us to go there and beat them for the second time in four days was a measure of our strength and belief.

It would have been interesting for the 1970 side to have played against the 1985 team. Two very good teams. Personally, I think the 1970 side would have had the edge, and have won six times out of ten. But then I am a little biased!

In 1987, Colin Harvey – the unassuming, childhood Evertonian – became manager of the club when Kendall left for pastures new in Spain. It was an honour he accepted reluctantly.

I didn't want to see Howard go. We had a great relationship and understanding, and I did not want to see it end. Actually, in 1986 there were reports that Howard was leaving for Barcelona and the board asked me if I was prepared to take over. Of course, I said yes, but that was with misgivings. Well, he never left for Spain then, but 12 months later he took the job with Atletico Bilbao and I was very proud to become manager. Here I was, the boy who worked his way through from the 'C' team, now managing the club. What an honour.

But Harvey's three-year tenure at the helm is not recalled by many fans with particular pleasure. One FA Cup final defeat (3–2 against the old enemy, Liverpool, in 1989) was all he really had to show for his efforts, plus a number of major signings who didn't quite come off. But Harvey vigorously defends his record in charge.

My big regret is that I didn't win anything. But during the three seasons I was manager we not only reached the Cup final, but also finished fourth, eighth and sixth in the league and reached the semi-final of the Littlewoods Cup. So, my record wasn't all that bad.

Still, failure to secure honours inevitably led to Harvey being sacked in November 1990 – only for him to return a few days later, as number two again under Howard Kendall!

I was out of work for five or six days. Then Howard rang me up and asked if I'd come back as his number two. I didn't even have to think about it. I was delighted. Everton were my first love, and that was it. Besides, it was a reunion of a partnership that worked so well in the '80s, and the one I never wanted to change. It was a bit strange for the players at first; after all I'd been their manager less than a week before, and now here I was, back in a different position. Some still called me 'Boss' for a while, but they soon got used to Howard being in charge. Remember, a lot of them were already there before Howard left in 1987.

This time, though, there was no magical reversal of Everton fortunes. The Kendall/Harvey alliance failed, for the first time either on the pitch or off it, to inspire success. Harvey says: 'We were both very disappointed at not being able to get things back on track. There were a lot of reasons for this, but the bottom line is that we didn't succeed.'

Kendall resigned in November 1993, with Harvey staying on for a couple more months before leaving. 'Mike Walker came in as manager, and he wanted to bring in his own people, which was fair enough, so I left in January 1994.'

Harvey was effectively out of football for five months, although he did do some scouting for Ipswich, at the request of their chief scout Charlie Woods.

> I saw lots of games, and kept myself fit by running ten miles every day. And then Andy King phoned me up and offered me a job with Mansfield. Now, I'd always got on with Andy, but I'd also just been approached by Sierra Leone in Africa to coach their Under-21 side. I had made my mind up to go, but they hadn't been back in touch with me. So I decided not to wait around and just took the Mansfield job as coach.

Harvey lived away from home for three or four nights a week in a hotel, in order to carry on his duties at Mansfield during the 1994–95 season, but after a few months he started to feel uneasy about his nomadic existence. Anxious to get back into the family home, he jumped at the chance to become Graeme Sharp's number two at Oldham.

> It was certainly tough at Oldham. Graeme didn't have a lot of money available for transfers, and the club wanted to develop their own youth policy. They certainly had some young players who weren't bad, but times just got tougher and tougher there, and eventually Graeme felt that he just couldn't do any more and left the club towards the end of the 1996–97 season. I left at the same time. Graeme did a good job under very difficult circumstances, but he just reached the point where he couldn't see things improving.

It was yet another former Evertonian who snapped up the experienced Harvey following his brief sojourn at Oldham. By this time, Adrian Heath was manager at Burnley and he gave Harvey a job on his backroom staff.

> Burnley was very different to Oldham. It has a good footballing

tradition, and is an area steeped in the game. There's enormous potential at the club, and I enjoyed my time there. In fact, I could easily have stayed a lot longer, but then I got a chance to go back to Everton . . .

In the summer of 1997, Harvey made an emotional return to Goodison when he was appointed as director of youth-team coaching. How strange that within weeks, he should be effectively reunited with Kendall, when the latter became manager of the club for a record third time! He says: 'Obviously Howard and I are not working as closely together as before, but it is good to be back with him at Everton.'

And, of course, no sooner had Harvey left Burnley than Heath followed him back to Goodison, being appointed as number two to Kendall – Harvey's old job.

Adrian's got a good footballing brain. He's very bright and I'm sure he will go far in the game. It's been very gratifying that I've had the chance to work with so many former Everton players in one capacity or another. People like Graeme and Adrian always did show a keen interest in the coaching side of the game. They'll do well.

Perhaps the reason that so many former Everton players are now employed on the managerial and coaching side of the game is a tribute to Harvey's own acumen and skill as a communicator. And as the game has truly become a global affair, with players of so many different nationalities involved with the English game, so a coach has to have increasing communication skills – or at least you'd have thought that was the case! Sometimes though, things can go a little awry over there, as Harvey found out for himself recently . . .

I went on an FA coaching course at the end of the 1996–97 season with Adrian Heath and another former Everton player from the '80s, Alan Harper. One of the lecturers was a chap called Gerard Houllier, who was technical director of the French FA. Now, his English is excellent. He taught in Liverpool for a while, married a girl from the city and has no problems being understood by English people. The FA told us not to bother taking notes, but to concentrate on what was being said. They would supply us all with notes within a month of the course. Fair enough. So anyway, a few weeks after the course finished, the notes from Houllier arrived . . . and they were in French! I don't know whether he had supplied the FA with French notes, or what, but they hadn't had them translated, and just sent them out! I had to get a friend of my daughter, who speaks fluent French, to translate them for me!

Such are the unexpected trials and tribulations of the coaching profession these days. But what does Harvey think about the way training and coaching methods have changed over the years?

There's no doubt that methods have become a lot more scientific. And people take a lot more notice about things such as diet, and also improving all-round strength. There has also been a considerable development on the psychological side of the game. Would the good players from the past have been able to cope with today's methods? Oh yes, I've got no doubts about that. They'd have adapted with little trouble.

Coaching is always evolving and developing – and it always did. I'm sure that it will continue to do so, as new methods are brought in. But then, the game itself is always changing as well. It's not necessarily better now than it was when I was playing, just different.

I always tell players: just enjoy your time in the game. I certainly did. My one regret as a player is that I wasn't able to go on longer.

Harvey has enjoyed a 35-year love affair, as a professional footballer, coach and manager, with Everton. Even during his brief spells away from the club, there never seemed any doubt where his heart and soul truly resided. Now he's back once again within the hallowed portals of Goodison Park, Colin Harvey – one of history's great Evertonians – has no intention of leaving. He says: 'I will be here as long as I'm wanted.'

Destiny earmarked Harvey for greatness at an early age. Despite the occasional set-backs, he can look back at a distinguished career that is almost unparalleled in helping to shape the modern history of Everton. That's no mean achievement for the local lad.

CHAPTER SEVEN

Adrian Heath

EVERTON PLAYING CAREER: 1981–1989
GAMES PLAYED: 293
GOALS SCORED: 89

Great things come in little packages, or so the story goes. In this case Everton had a player who burst on to the scene with great expectations. At first Adrian did not exactly set the world on fire. Howard Kendall kept faith in him, and Adrian, in many people's eyes, changed the course of Everton's history by scoring a decisive goal in a Milk Cup match against Oxford United in 1983. When he joined the club it was four days before his 21st birthday.

It was the best birthday present I ever had. Howard was the manager that bought me and to think I actually played with Howard when he was at Stoke City. We go back a long way from when I was 16. I had played about 120 games for Stoke before Everton came in for me. For me it was a fantastic feeling knowing that I was wanted by Everton because I was an Everton fan from the age of seven even though I was living in Stoke. I used to watch Stoke both home and away, but my other favourite team was Everton. The reason I liked Everton, and I know it might seem a bit silly, was because of those arches behind the goals they had in those days. And I also loved the goal that Andy King scored against Liverpool at Goodison, when Andy got pushed off the pitch by a policeman when he was interviewed after the game. And of course everybody remembers Eddie Cavanagh running on to the pitch when he dropped his jacket in the '66 Cup final. All in all, I don't know whether it was the underdog thing when I was growing up as to why I loved the club, but I always remember going to Goodison when Stoke played there and I just loved the place. My dad used to go on about the '60s team with Ball, Harvey and Kendall and how great they were.

Adrian arrived at Goodison for a fee of £700,000. At the time it was a club record transfer fee. He was an attacking midfielder who could handle a striker's role whenever the need arose. In his first year, Adrian found it hard work.

I was not playing particularly well. We were a very young side at the time and we all found it a little bit difficult to cope with the pressure and expectations of such a big club. We found it tough to make a real breakthrough. We did believe in ourselves but we just couldn't get it right. We needed experience alongside us. Every team has to have one or two experienced heads. In fact I remember my début for Everton against Southampton. I was playing against Alan Ball. I remember the headline saying that I was the new Ball. That didn't help. I mean, to be the club's record signing and then have that heaped upon your shoulders, it was a bit much.

Added to that, we were not a particularly good side. I was, I suppose, one of the earlier pieces of the jigsaw that would go on to make a big splash in the league. Now when I look back it's fantastic to know that I played a part in the team that went on to become the most successful side in the club's history. I think the 1969–70 team was the next best side. They were something special. I'll always remember Alan Whittle coming into the team and going on to score a load of goals in such a short space of time. I loved Alan Ball and the way he played, but having worked with both Colin and Howard, I couldn't believe how good they were still, all those years later. I mean, Colin had a plastic hip and he was still the best player in training. Whenever we played five-a-side or eight across the pitch and whoever was picking the teams, I always thought they were creeping to the boss, but really they were the best players. I used to think what a team they must have been to play against.

Adrian scored his first goal against Brighton in an away game in 1981. However Everton lost 3–1. He scored six goals in his first season and Everton finished eighth in the table. The next season saw Everton in mid-table for the first part of the season and then climb to finish seventh. The following season saw Everton plummet to the relegation zone. Adrian found it hard to work out why Everton were, at the time, on such a bad run.

I think it was an accumulation of a lot of things. I think if people had seen us playing from Monday to Friday in training and seen the sort of quality that we produced, the sort of quality that people were to see a season and a half later, then they too would have not been able to work out why we looked poor in competitive matches. I think that we were all young lads, perhaps a little bit inhibited by the fact that we were playing for such a big club that meant we wouldn't force ourselves on the opposition or the games themselves. That's why the signings of Peter Reid and Andy Gray were so important. They brought the stability and their vast experience to the team. Who knows, had we been able to just fight on and survive that season, we might have found the belief in ourselves the following season.

By December 1983, Howard had come under increasing pressure to resign as manager. It was not the best of times for all concerned. The players were trying their best for Howard, but it didn't seem to work. The reaction of Howard towards the players back then was typical of the man.

The best comment I could say about Howard at that time was that never did he once turn on the players, or use us as an excuse. He always believed in the set of players he had around him. After all we were the ones who were letting him down. He was the one tearing his hair out, which probably explains why he's bald now. The greatest thing was he never gave up on us. He never said, 'Well, they've had their chance, get rid of them and we'll get some new players in'. He just had this fantastic belief in us. It's a lesson I've taken into management now. In the end his belief paid off. Even if it hadn't, we would still have been grateful to him for having such patience with us.

That belief in the players really began to pay off even if it was a little fortuitous. In January 1984, Everton went to Oxford United for the quarter-final of the Milk Cup competition. It was a game that most people had expected Everton to lose given their current form.

That was an important game for Everton. Although the goal I scored, to me, was not the most important one. I reckon it was the FA Cup tie against Stoke when Andy Gray scored, because that was a game we had to win to try and begin to believe in ourselves, especially after the rotten result against Coventry at home previously. That game was probably the one that convinced us that we might have turned the corner. Then we

followed it up against Oxford to set up the replay. People underestimated
the great performances of Oxford that year. If I remember rightly they
had knocked out Leeds, Newcastle and Arsenal and we were expected to
be the next big club to go. It was never going to be easy. They had a mean
bunch of players, but we dug in and made life difficult for them and then
Kevin Brock hit that backpass that let me in. It wasn't an easy goal
because the pitch at that end was bone hard and I struggled to keep my
feet, but I somehow managed to squeeze it past the keeper. Then of
course we got them back at Goodison where we won 4–1. By then I
sensed that we were off and running then in terms of form. From then on
I don't think we lost that many games.

In fact Everton only lost five more matches that season including the
second leg of the Milk Cup semi-final against Aston Villa. Even then, they
still went on to win the tie and go on to Wembley to face the old enemy,
Liverpool, in the first-ever Wembley showdown between the two clubs.

That is a day I'll never ever forget. It was a fantastic sight seeing the blue
and red colours everywhere. As for the match, I still think to this day that
we were robbed. We should have won the game. Alan Hansen handled
the ball as I had turned it towards the goal. Alan was the last man on the
line so it would certainly have gone in. It was so clear even the TV
cameras saw it. However, it wasn't to be and they went and beat us in the
replay at Maine Road. But it was a very special occasion all the same. It
was billed as the friendly final, but I'll tell you what, it was definitely not
friendly on the pitch. In all the derby games I've played none was as
passionate as that one. The good thing about derby matches is that both
teams play as if their lives depended on them, but afterwards we all mix
socially. We nearly all lived in the same area so we were bound to see
each other. In fact Sammy Lee is still a good friend to this day.

The 1984–85 season was looked forward to by everyone at the club.
Everton had won the FA Cup and the feeling was that this was the season
that Everton could at last realise all the potential that Howard Kendall
always believed was there.

I know, from speaking to other people in the game, that at that time we
were very, very hard to play against, because the one thing that side had
was that we could do everything that was expected in each game. We
could tackle, pass accurately and take our chances at the right times. We

had players that, if need be, could look after themselves, which is a mark of a top-class side, which we were.

One of the games that epitomised the season was the game against Manchester United when we won 5–0. The good thing about that day was that we epitomised all that we were good at. We were hard-working, very determined and dogged when we didn't have the ball, and when we needed to play attractive football, we played some of the best football that I had ever known. In fact some of my friends have often said that the football that season was the best that they had ever witnessed.

Adrian was showing his best form since joining the club. Then in December, Adrian played against Sheffield Wednesday at Goodison. A tackle by Brian Marwood left Adrian in agony and the resulting injury ruled him out of the rest of that historic season.

I remember being told by Bobby Robson that I would be in the next England squad. I was absolutely delighted. It would have been at Old Trafford on the Wednesday, but I did my knee in on the Saturday. I've never really spoken about it much, but recently I was talking to Peter Reid and he said that he half blamed himself as he reckoned that his pass was a bit short. I remember that I did have to come back to it. Then instead of basically playing it off, I tried to let the ball run past me and block the player off. The next thing I know Brian came through me and had taken everything. It was very disappointing.

People have told me that I was never really the same after that season. I beg to differ a little bit. I may have lost a little bit of zip in my running, but I went on to win the Championship a couple of years later and have a good career after leaving Everton. The biggest disappointment for me though was missing the European Cup Winners' Cup final in Rotterdam. I remember vividly sitting in the main stand. In fact Mark Higgins was with me. He too had a very bad injury that season. The one thing that I had done all through the season was to be involved as much as possible with the team. I went to every game that the team played, even if it meant travelling on my own. Howard was very good to me allowing me to travel with the lads. I felt involved as I was in the dressing-room and on the bench so that I was close to the action. That particular night, for security reasons and with it being in a foreign country, they only allowed so many passes into the dressing-room area and in other areas around the ground. So as I sat there, it really hit me what that injury had robbed me of. To be honest, I would rather have sat in the stand, where all the

Everton fans were behind the goal, than sit with the dignitaries in the Main stand, watching the lads go out there and win the Cup. I just never felt part of it. I don't think I have ever felt so lost as I did that night.

Adrian came back slowly but surely the following season. The doubts had set in about whether he would be the same player.

It was such a bad injury even I had my doubts as to playing top-flight football. What I didn't know was that my surgeon was saying to me that the operation was a big success, but privately he was telling the club that I would be lucky if I ever played at all, never mind professionally again. Howard, Colin and the players kept encouraging me and I will be forever indebted to John Clinkard, the physiotherapist, as he used to spend morning, noon and night with me. I remember having treatment at eight o'clock in the morning through to nine, ten o'clock at night at Bellefield. It was a hard slog, but it was important to me to have everybody encouraging me at that time. The supporters were fabulous to me as well. Therefore I was determined to get back into the first team as they saw the best of me just before my injury.

In the 1985–86 season Adrian felt a bit frustrated. He was now back in the team, but he was played in a variety of positions in order to accommodate Everton's new signing, Gary Lineker.

That was a funny time for me. I was in the team, but I was not able to play at my best because of the different positions I played in. Gary had come to the club and it was a question of how do I fit into the pattern. It's certainly not a personal thing with Gary, indeed I have spoken to him about it on occasions, but despite him scoring 40 goals that season, which is a great achievement in itself, the fact was we won nothing at the end of the day. I thought the overall shape of the side suffered. I think Gary scored so many goals that other people couldn't score.

If you look at the following season the goals were shared around the team. I got 15, Derek Mountfield got 15, Graeme Sharp scored 15. I personally take a great deal of satisfaction that we won the League that season as I felt I had been proved right all along.

After winning the League in the 1986–87 season, boss Howard Kendall left Everton to try his luck in Europe. Colin Harvey was the new manager. Adrian now had to think about his own future.

When Colin came in, I got the feeling that he wanted to change the team around a little bit. He wanted to bring in one or two new people. An opportunity to play in Spain came up and it was something that I had always wanted to do. At the time I thought it was the right decision both for Everton and for me personally. I joined Español and I never regretted the decision. The lifestyle was different and so was the football. I learned a lot from Javier Clemente, the coach, and I stayed there for a season.

Looking back on his Everton career, Adrian remembers that one of the ingredients of the success that came to the club was that the dressing-room was filled with characters who would probably have been quite at home in a cabaret line-up.

There were many characters when I was there. However, when Neville came to the club you couldn't get a peep out of him. He hardly spoke and it was hard work to get any opinion out of him. Now look at him! Whenever he speaks now it will more often than not make a lot of sense, but every once in a while he will drop a bombshell into the conversation. We had a very lively dressing-room with Andy Gray and Peter Reid. John Bailey was always ribbing one of us. People have known me by my nickname of Inchy, but to be honest I was called that from a very early age. I was always the smallest in the class at school. It was just one of those things that stuck and naturally with that lot in the dressing-room I was always going to be called Inchy.

For me Andy and Peter had such an influence on the rest of us. They acted as a catalyst in terms of the success that the club achieved. To think that they both failed the medical when we signed them. Again that was another plus for Howard when he pushed those transfers through. As I say to my players now, the best players are not always the ones with the best ability, it's the ones that produce the football skills week in week out and then affect other people in the way they play. I well remember the amount of times that Andy would rip into me at half-time when he felt I wasn't doing myself justice in the game. Reidy just wouldn't forgive you if you weren't prepared to get stuck in. They were two terrific players. I loved playing with them.

The one who came through who really turned it on for me was Trevor Steven. He had everything you want in a player. He had pace, a change in direction, he was intelligent and he had two good feet and was good in the air. Gary Stevens was a great athlete. But there is one player I always mention when talking about Everton at that time, who had a bit of a reputation mainly for the wrong reasons and that was Pat Van Den Hauwe. I honestly believe when we won that championship in 1986–87, he was our best player. He hardly ever had a bad game for Everton and he was an integral part of that side that sometimes gets overlooked. What was significant about that season was that as a team we would always have a go at each other on the pitch, but it was always for the good of the team. There was nothing personal about it. After the game we would go for a pint and be just as friendly as usual. We were a great team scoring great goals with a great will to win. I loved it there and it will always be a special part of my life.

I scored some important goals and ones that I was very pleased with. I remember one at Norwich, where Neville kicked it upfield to me on the halfway line and I just flicked it up over the defender and then I volleyed it in. The other one that I will probably be always remembered for was the semi-final one against Southampton in 1984 at Highbury. It was the one I will always look back on with the most happiness and joy. It was something I'll never forget, the look on the supporters' faces was fantastic. I remember Howard saying that the coach-driver would get the sack if he got the team back home before four o'clock in the morning. It was the slowest coach journey I've ever known! It was that good Terry Darracott got hold of the mike and started singing. We used to call him Radio Tex as he loved his music. That night he invited the lads to join him to sing all sorts.

In Spain it was so different for me. For one I couldn't even speak the language. So, from being in such a lively dressing-room at Goodison to becoming the one who sits in the corner watching all the banter flying around, I thought I'd better get the language sorted out, otherwise it would be a long time before I would be able to get on with the job. I loved the football out there. It was very different to the way I had always played. It was more technical and I had a little bit more time and space. There was a little bit more emphasis on keeping the ball and not giving it away as much. The biggest mistake I made was not staying out there longer.

Adrian came back to join Aston Villa. He felt he played well after his Spanish times, but it was a case of rebuilding for Villa, and he left to join Howard Kendall at Manchester City. When he arrived there it was just like old times as there were several ex-Everton players there too.

When Howard took over at City they were sixth from bottom. They finished the season sixth from top. Howard bought well when he was there. Niall Quinn was a player nobody seemed to want to touch, but Howard liked him and took that gamble. Fortunately it paid off. It was like being back at Everton what with me, Alan Harper, Neil Pointon and Peter Reid. I must admit at times it was a bit embarrassing as it was like an Everton reserves' team, and we got a bit of stick for that. But, I think if you look at City now, they haven't really recovered since Howard left them, therefore nobody can complain about the players Howard bought.

Whilst at Manchester City, Adrian got the opportunity to go back to Stoke City on loan which he relished. He was back with the team that he used to watch as a boy. He is very proud that he went to Wembley with them to play in the Auto Glass Trophy final. The following season he went to Burnley. He played for two and a half years at Burnley before once again he rejoined Howard Kendall at Sheffield United. By now his playing career was coming to an end and Adrian started to look at the management side of life.

I always knew I would want to go into management. From a very young age that was something I always wanted to do. I was forever talking about football, even as a lad, and when the opportunity came up at Burnley, I just had to go for it. Here I could begin to put my own thoughts across. I would have liked to have stayed with Howard for a couple more years to learn a lot more, but I probably would never had got the opportunity to manage such a good club as this. I like to think I have picked up a lot from my various managers throughout my career, mainly Howard for obvious reasons. I was fortunate to play for Javier Clemente in Spain who has the best reputation there. He is very much in the Brian Clough mould, very abrasive and controversial, but a terrific person to work for and I got on very well with him and I still do to this day.

It is a challenge to manage a club like Burnley where you have to be conscious of the amount of money that you can spend on players. Having said that, though, I think all managers today have to watch what they spend. It is more difficult in today's climate as supporters don't give managers enough time to build something that in the long term will end up successful. The greater the expectation from the fans, the less time you seem to have. Where I am at the moment, Burnley have under-achieved for the last 25 to 30 years, but I believe that we have the capability to become a first division side pretty soon. For instance I don't think the likes of Coventry are any bigger than Burnley given the size and potential of the club. Obviously they have survived in the top division and now Sky TV give them a lot of money, which helps them stay there to a certain extent. However, when it comes to potential for Burnley, I would say that we would get just as many coming to see us, if not more, than they already get at the likes of Coventry. Now it's up to me to get the club moving in the right direction in order to achieve those targets.

My job is made easier in some respects as I wanted to move down a division in order to make it work to the best of my ability, and I suppose the players here will look up to me because of the success I have achieved over the years. Remember, I could have stayed with Sheffield United in the first division in the hope that they would be in the Premiership, but I felt that I could do something really good here at Burnley. Talking about the respect that one can get at a lower division club, I've got a player here, David Eyres, who is a massive Evertonian and can remember more of my goals at Everton than I can. So it helps that players know about me and my reputation in the game.

Adrian Heath will always be remembered for his darting little runs and his little one-twos that would always seem to come off as Everton marched on to glory. He is still fondly remembered as Inchy by the fans – yet another hero amongst a whole host of them in the mid-'80s teams.

Since we interviewed him for this book, Adrian has gone full circle and returned to the club that brought him so much success and pleasure. He is now assistant manager to none other than Howard Kendall. As he mentioned earlier, he wished he had spent more time with Howard learning a few more tricks of the trade. Now he hopes to be able to bring the good times back to Goodison. As you can tell, he won't be happy until he's achieved that.

CHAPTER EIGHT

Dave Hickson

EVERTON PLAYING CAREER: 1948–1955 and 1957–1959
GAMES PLAYED: 243
GOALS SCORED: 111

The number nine shirt has always been the most revered at Everton. Dean, Lawton, Royle, Gray, Sharp, Ferguson . . . The list of legends who have graced the shirt is seemingly endless. And into this category the dynamic Dave Hickson fits very well. He was a Goodison hero during the tough times in the 1950s, when trophies were very thin on the ground and under-achievement was the name of the game. 'My first memory of the club?' he says. 'That was when I came here whilst I was still at school, and it was impressive even back then.'

And in 1948, after scoring goals for local side Ellesmere Port, Hickson joined Everton at the age of 18, although his immediate progress was interrupted by the inevitable call to national service. While serving his country, however, Hickson was fortunate to receive coaching instructions from arguably the greatest goalscorer English football has ever known – none other than 'Dixie' Dean!

I was in the Cheshire Army Cadets at the time and 'Dixie' was doing some coaching for the side, and actually being able to talk to him and learn was just invaluable. He was an amazing character, and if you couldn't pick up hints and ideas from him, then you had no chance.

But Dean wasn't the only legend whom the young Hickson encountered during his early tenure at Goodison.

Joe Mercer, such a great wing-half, was still there when I first joined, and so was that superb defender T.G. Jones. In fact, the place just seemed stuffed with great names to me. And one of the biggest characters was a guy called Alex Stevenson, an inside-forward who joined the club the season after they won the FA Cup in 1933. He was a real comedian. Every club had their comic back then, probably still do, someone who breaks the monotony and always has a joke to tell, and Alex was ours. Mind you, there was more to him than just a few jokes. He was a brilliant player as well! He scored nearly a century of goals for the club either side of the Second World War [the actual tally was 90].

Hickson finally got his chance in the Blues first team in September 1951, against Leeds. How strange that the man he took over from in the team was a journeyman player of no consequence; someone, however, who went on to make a name for himself in the manager's chair at Goodison: Harry Catterick.

> Finally getting a chance of first-team football was just fantastic for me, even though we were a second division team back then. It didn't matter, I was just happy to be following in the footsteps of 'Dixie' and Tommy Lawton. What a tradition to live up to!

But Hickson took it all in his stride, forging a partnership with John Willie Parker that was to terrorise second division defences over the next few years. The stylish, rapier thrusts of Parker complemented neatly the powerhouse, explosive style of Hickson, as the latter earned a reputation for putting his head in where others would fear to put even the boot. In fact, on one famous FA Cup occasion, Hickson cut open his head twice in the same afternoon. It was 1953. The fifth round at Goodison Park against Man United. The ebullient striker needed stitches in a gashed eyebrow early on, but returned to score the winning goal, and then re-opened the wound a little later. However, in the days before substitutes were introduced into the game, players would only leave the field in a coffin. Hickson, blood streaming down his face, stayed on – and promptly transformed himself into a folk hero.

Sadly, that FA Cup run ended against Bolton in the semi-finals, but a year later Hickson blasted 25 goals as Everton raced out of the second division and made provisions to re-impose themselves as a force to be reckoned with.

However, if the dynamic centre-forward had hopes of establishing himself as a star in the top flight, they were soon dashed. Much to his disappointment, manager Cliff Britton let him go in 1955 to Aston Villa, for a fee of £17,500. But the Merseysider was unable to settle away from Everton. He played a dozen times for Villa before going to Huddersfield, where Bill Shankly was starting to make an impact. But again wanderlust stopped his development and, after making just 54 appearances in two seasons, he was delighted and somewhat surprised when the new Everton manager Ian Buchan brought him back to his spiritual home for just £7,500 in August 1957.

The fans were as pleased to see their old combative hero back as was the man himself to be in a blue shirt once more. But after two years he found himself surplus to requirements once more. New boss Johnny Carey was starting to build for the future and decided that the ageing Hickson no longer fitted in.

I didn't want to leave Everton again, but if you're not wanted what can you do? However, I made it plain that if I had to leave Everton to carry on playing, then okay I'd do that, but I did not want to leave the city of Liverpool. And so I ended up crossing Stanley Park and going to Anfield. It was a bit strange, but at least I was still in the city I loved.

Everton fans, though, were furious that Carey had, in November 1959, allowed their hero to cross over and play for the dreaded enemy even although the Anfield crew were then in the second division. But at least with the divisional difference Hickson didn't have to play against his beloved Everton during his two years at Anfield.

After leaving Liverpool, the tireless battler had spells with non-league Cambridge City and Bury, before ending his playing days in England by returning to Merseyside to join Tranmere. And in doing so, he made a little piece of history by becoming the first player ever to play first-team football for all three senior clubs on Merseyside.

In 1964, Hickson was tempted over to Northern Ireland, where he became player-manager of Ballymena United. It was a different standard of football, one far below what he had been accustomed to, but it did provide Hickson with a chance to start out on what he hoped would be a distinguished managerial career.

The flare-up of the Troubles in the late '60s prompted me to return from Northern Ireland. It suddenly became very dangerous. So I came back home and applied for a few coaching and management jobs, but nothing materialised. So I had to go out and work for a living!

Hickson worked for the environmental health department at Ellesmere Port, and turned out on a part-time basis for the local team. He had come full circle.

Now retired, the silver-haired lion of Goodison still plays an active role in promotional work for the club. He says: 'I do a lot on the community side for Everton. It's a part-time job but I still thoroughly enjoy being involved with all that's happening.' He has even been known to turn out in the blue of Everton for charity and celebrity matches. He may be well into his 60s, but there's still a hunger and steel about Hickson that few defenders would like to face.

Hickson might have enjoyed spells at a number of clubs, but there's no doubting where his allegiances lie. He says: 'I've always said that I'd break every bone in my body for any club I played for, but I'd have died for Everton. That's how much the club means to me.'

Hickson was unlucky never to be capped by England – a combination of Everton's lack of success at the time and the presence of goalscoring immortals such as Stan Mortenson kept him from receiving national honours. He still sits proudly as one of only five post-war Everton strikers to have notched up more than a century of goals for the club. And only Graeme Sharp, Bob Latchford and Joe Royle actually managed to top his 111 goals. Who knows, if he had played in another era perhaps he'd have beaten the lot.

CHAPTER NINE

Jimmy Husband

EVERTON PLAYING CAREER: 1964–1974
GAMES PLAYED: 197
GOALS SCORED: 55

When one thinks of the glory times in the '60s, one person who comes to mind as having played a very important part in that era was Jimmy Husband. Jimmy was loved by the fans for his skill and pace. The sight of Jimmy running at defences always had the Goodison crowd purring with delight. An attacking player, Jimmy showed skill way beyond his years at times. He was unpredictable, which meant the opposition often didn't know how to shackle him. Always keen to have a go when a half chance presented itself, Jimmy will always be remembered as a flamboyant player who any team would want on their side.

Jimmy joined straight from school and became a professional player in October 1964. Everton were just one of 18 clubs chasing his signature and probably won the race to sign him on the strength of the fact that they were the glamour club of the time. The players there were some of the greats in British football and he wanted to be a part of the team. At the time of joining, Jimmy had already been playing with England Schoolboys, so it was no wonder there was a lot of competition for his signature.

It was very impressive. I was seeing all these great players on a daily basis, people like Tony Kay, Alex Young and so on. As a 15-year-old kid I was very excited by it all. The only trouble was I was very homesick. The club were great about sorting out my digs and I also had a special deal with Everton in that they paid once a month for me to go home on the train back to Newcastle. It wasn't all pleasant, though, as they were very strict in those days as well. You had to be turned out well and be on time for training. Harry Catterick was very good to us youth players. I think he realised that he had some very good ones coming through. He didn't speak to you on a personal basis, but he was always around.

Jimmy made his full début in the second to last game of the 1964–65 season, away at Fulham.

> If I remember rightly it was a bank holiday weekend when the Boat Race was on. I had played on that Saturday in the reserves and had listened to the race and gone back to my digs when I got a phone call. Everton had played at home that day and Derek Temple had picked up an injury. I was told to get to Goodison as quickly as I could. I told them I was getting the bus, and they said not to and that they would send Harry Cooke, the chief scout, to come and pick me up. I had a little carrier bag with all my stuff in and off we went. I played against Fulham on the Monday. I was looked after by the players on the pitch that day. We drew 1–1 and I was pleased to have got that out of the way.

For the next few years Jimmy was brought into the first team whenever there were injuries to others. He saw himself very much as a reserve player as he was still very young. By 1967, a lot of the senior players had moved on, which left gaps in the team enabling Jimmy and others to come into the team on a regular basis. Jimmy made a great impact on the fans when he started to play regularly and was the second-highest scorer for Everton in the 1968–69 season, with 19 goals, behind Joe Royle who finished on 22. In that season Everton played Derby County in a League Cup match which ended in a 0–0 draw. Dave Mackay was seen as very much the villain that day as he lunged at Jimmy and was extremely late in the tackle. He didn't even get booked, which annoyed the crowd. People were starting to wonder whether that tackle had finished off a very promising career. However, Jimmy bounced back to silence them and went on to score his 19 goals that season. By now, Jimmy was regarded by many at the club as being one of the new star players and the younger ones coming up through the ranks were now looking up to him.

> I remember one player in particular who went on to play and captain the team and that was Mick Lyons. I wasn't impressed with him at first when he was playing for the youth team. He just looked awkward and gangly but he was quick as well. Whenever there were races in training Mick would always seem to win, which I couldn't understand because he

looked like he just wouldn't be able to run effectively, but he kept doing it. He had great stamina. He wasn't a sprinter, but anything over a mile no one could touch him. His touch on the ball when he was young was not particularly good but he went and proved everyone wrong. Alan Whittle was another one I noticed and in the end we both were challenging for the same place in the team.

The following season, 1969–70, Everton won the championship. For Jimmy the season had gone very well until he was injured towards the end of the campaign. Alan Whittle came in and went on a phenomenal scoring run which kept Jimmy out of the team when he had regained his fitness.

That was very disappointing for me – the way we won the championship. I had played 30-odd games and then I got injured and Alan Whittle got my place. To be fair, though, he scored 11 goals in 15 games and you can't drop someone who is banging them in like that. It was great winning a championship medal though. The following season I knew that Alan and I were going to have to battle it out as to who was to start the season. They chose Alan to begin with and I wasn't very happy and I asked for a transfer and that was refused. By the third game I was back in, as Alan could not pick up from where he left off. I started scoring again until I got another injury. From then on Alan and I shared the place in the side. As far as I was concerned, I was happy to be playing whenever, and I actually liked playing as an old-fashioned inside-forward.

What killed that idea, of course, was when England won the World Cup with the 4–3–3 formation. From then on every team changed their way of thinking. All of a sudden, from having five forwards, teams had to try and accommodate them all in a new formation which wasn't going to happen. It was Harry's decision to move me to an outside position to cut in and support the central striker. Harry saw that I was quick and knew he could get me to run either down the wing or cut inside and become a support to the other forwards. Because I was quick I did pick up quite a few injuries. I think nowadays training methods have improved so that somebody like me will not get injured as much.

In talking to Jimmy for this book, we learned that there were great characters at the club. There was one that came as a bit of a surprise to us.

One player who was a great character and who a lot of the ex-players tend to forget when talking about such people, is Ray Wilson. He impressed me a lot. He was a lot older than me. I had great respect for him as he was an England international, a stylish player. He did things that seemed to a 19-year-old like me, at the time, very different to what us younger players did. He smoked a pipe for a start. He wore different clothes to the rest of us. He used to take the mickey out of my clothes as I was wearing the type of clothes that the Rolling Stones were wearing at the time. He would wear stuff the like of which Tony Bennett or Frank Sinatra would wear.

Brian Labone was like the father of the team. He was considered the man to lead the team by Harry Catterick. Today it seems that the captain is the best player in more cases than not. In those days the captaincy was given to the player who could influence the rest of the team in the way that the manager wanted. He would be the wise head, I suppose. Brian got on well with the youngsters and the rest of the players.

We also had other characters at the club which not many fans knew about. People like one of my first trainers, Ron Lewin. I didn't particularly like him as he was such a disciplinarian and he would push us, in my opinion, a bit too hard, but he was a skilful coach.

Jimmy recalls the time just over a season after Everton won the League in 1970.

It was a horrendous time for the club, really. Harry had a heart attack, the team was crumbling after we had been one of the best sides in England. I had a feeling that it was not going to be corrected for a long time. Since I had been there, Everton were one of the top four teams in the country and here it was all falling apart. At one point Tommy Casey became top man at the club while Harry was recovering. He was the youth-team coach when I joined and all of a sudden he was taking charge of the team. Brian Labone, I think, had retired or was just about to, and the players just couldn't get it right on the pitch and so the results suffered. Mind you we were not the only club to build a winning team and then watch as it all fell apart. In fact Liverpool were the first team to build on their successes in the '70s. Liverpool were also the first to promote from within. Normally, clubs would sack a manager and get another one in and he would start again building a squad, but with Liverpool they started the continuity of promoting from within and therefore the squad would not change as much. What seemed to happen with us was that Harry left and Billy Bingham came in and sold Colin Harvey, Joe Royle

and me amongst others, so Everton didn't have a settled squad for quite
some time.

When Billy Bingham took over in May 1973, Jimmy felt that Billy wanted
his own players so that the team was fresh. Jimmy didn't get to play too
many times after Billy was made the manager and it wasn't long before
other clubs were interested in signing him. Luton Town, under manager
Harry Haslam, signed him in November 1973 and Jimmy was looking
forward to playing first-team football regularly again.

It wasn't so much of a wrench to leave Everton, because I could see that
things were brewing and that it wasn't going to be the same for me at all.
In a strange way I was looking forward to a change. I felt as if I needed
a change as well as Everton. I had been there since the age of 15. I was
now 28 and it was the right decision. Thankfully, for me it worked out
really well. I had four great years at Luton and I felt I did well for them.
I was leading goalscorer for two or three of the years I was there. We
were promoted back into the first division, which for a small team like
Luton was brilliant.

Of course there was a hell of a difference in the two clubs. I was used
to Bellefield training ground. Luton didn't possess their own training
ground. We used to train at places like the Co-op grounds. We were
begging and borrowing off anyone who could help in that area.
Companies that had social clubs also had us training on their grounds. It
was a major culture shock, to say the least. I went to Luton last year to
watch a match and they have spent a lot of money since my days there
on all sorts of facilities for the staff. When I was there, there were two
old dressing-rooms with wooden floors. Nobody had their own peg or
locker or anything like that. It was very basic. But it was a good squad
and a happy one.

There were some great players coming through like Andy King and
Peter Anderson, who were excellent players. Of course, we had the
Futcher twins who were terrific. Paul should have gone on to play for
England but it never happened for him. I got on well with the manager,
Harry Haslam. He was the total opposite of Catterick. Catterick was God
and not approachable whereas Harry Haslam was the sort that would say,
'Jimmy, can you pop up to my office whenever you are ready. Just a
quick word' and so on. Then I would go up to his room and just have a
chat and a cup of tea and some biscuits. He smoked like a trooper and
was a great comedian. He knew every joke that was going and had a

great delivery too. He should have been a professional comedian really. A great character within the game. I was sorry to see him go. Harry left the club over some financial matter and David Pleat took over.

David had been at the club for quite a while. He had been just a clerk in the office for most of that time. Us senior pros just couldn't help but to call him Dave as opposed to Boss. One day I got a phone call, out of the blue, from the ex-Chelsea defender Eddie McCreadie. He had just accepted a job in America as a coach with Memphis. He had called David up and asked about me, and David gave him permission to speak to me. John Faulkner, the Luton captain, also came over with me, which was good, so I didn't feel I was on my own. The two families got on well and it was a lot easier for me. I stayed at Memphis for two years. There were other players I knew, people like Alan Birchnall and Charlie Cooke, who had also played for Chelsea.

Life in America was very different for Jimmy. The facilities were second to none. The home ground was a stadium that could hold 60,000 people. Unfortunately, the Americans' interest in football evaporated quickly. They couldn't understand the game at that time and it was all too slow and not high scoring enough for them. In the first of those two years, the New York Cosmos were the champions and had the third-highest home average attendance in the soccer world.

To give you an idea about how little the supporters knew about the game, every week in the matchday programme they would print articles about what happens at a free kick and what a throw-in was and stuff like that. It was really weird playing to people that hadn't got a clue what the game of soccer was about. Memphis averaged 10,000 people coming to the games, which was about the same as what Luton were getting. It was a great experience and it was fabulous for my kids. We would finish training at about midday, which was the same as in England, but we would always be training in shorts and the weather was magnificent. After training we would go back home and go out to loads of fun places with the family, which you never tended to do in England, partly because of the weather and the fact that in England, at that time, they didn't have things like amusement parks.

After two years in Memphis, Jimmy was on the move again. Again it came through Eddie McCreadie.

What happened was that Eddie had left the club. The franchise had run out and the club was bought out by a multi-billionaire from Calgary in Canada, and therefore the team was going to be uprooted to Calgary. I didn't want to move as I had my son settled in school and I didn't want a complete change at that time. So for a few months I did nothing but just enjoy myself. Eddie hadn't gone to Calgary either and he had taken a job in Cleveland, Ohio, in an indoor league. He then invited me to go up there and join him. I had one season playing in the indoor soccer, which I believe is still pretty big today, but I hated it. You spend all your life playing the professional game and then all of a sudden I was being paid to play six-a-side. It was more like ice hockey only you are using a football instead of a stick and a puck. I was constantly being bashed against the boards.

There were some players there that had been playing for a while and technically they were very good, but underneath they were useless really. If they had been playing on a full-size pitch they would probably not have been able to get into Hartlepool's team. Yet in the indoor soccer league they were major stars. They knew that all they had to do was smack the ball against the boards next to the goal and get the rebounds into the net. I didn't know about all that crap. To completely relearn how to play that version of football was just too much. I just wanted to get away.

Then, again out of the blue, I got a phone call from Brian Harvey, Colin Harvey's brother. He had been in America for a while coaching a soccer team in Oklahoma. There was a new American league being set up as competition to the NASL. I was not going to get great money for playing, but I thought, yes, I'll give it a go. I was getting to the end of my career anyway, so I ended up for my last two years in Oklahoma. I actually could have gone on for another season or two, but the owner had a chain of supermarkets and he went bust. We had got three-quarters of the way through the season and we were not getting our wages. I remember one time I was complaining like hell to him and in the end he just signed this form and said, 'Go to one of my supermarkets and just get what you want.' So my wife and I go to the supermarket with two of these huge trolleys and we stacked them as high as we could and took them home. After that I just said to my family that we were getting out of there. It had become a joke. I told Brian and he understood and then we got the next flight home.

The year was now 1983. Jimmy was at a bit of a loose end and at first he didn't do very much at all. He had to decide whether or not to try to get a job in football. He was not then that keen on becoming a coach, which is something that he regrets to this day. He has seen quite a few friends make a lucrative living out of that side of football. He even admits to being a bit jealous of them.

I felt that I could have contributed my experience to the game but it never happened. So, whilst we were in America, the house that I still had over here, in the village just outside Luton, was rented out. There was an American forces base about four miles away and I rented it out to them so that officers could stay in a decent place while over here. When I came back, of course, I had to give them six months notice. So for that time we lived in Liverpool with my mother-in-law. While I was there I decided to catch up with a lot of people I hadn't seen for years and do very little. I think the expression that people use today for what I was doing then is 'chilling out'. After I had done that I wanted to move back into my home.

I thought that I needed to do something so, like a lot of footballers, I had a pub for two years. I wanted to buy my own pub, which I did, in a lovely little village called Roxton in North Bedfordshire. I had only been there for two years when the *Liverpool Echo* ran a little story about me. What had happened was that I was still fit as I used to run for four miles every day. Some bloke came into the pub one day and asked me if I wanted to play for his team. I said that I didn't really want to be bothered with all that again. I had been offered loads of local teams but I had turned them all down. He then said that I might want to consider playing for this one and I asked him why. He said that they were called Everton. Apparently there was a village, about three miles from where we had bought the pub, called Everton. Anyway, the *Liverpool Echo* did a big story on it, and I still have the clippings of it, with the headline saying something like, 'Former star rejoins Everton.' I thought Everton must have wet themselves when they saw that.

After he had sold the pub tenancy, Jimmy did some coaching work for a counties team and he started to think about whether to go into that side of the game. As there wasn't much money in local coaching, he decided against it.

After I had told the brewery that I was selling the tenancy, I had to wait six months for it all to go through. One day this chap came in and heard about me leaving the pub and said to me that there might be a job going in the company he worked for, Godfrey Davis, the car hire company.

What had happened was that someone was retiring and it coincided with me leaving the pub business. I became next in line to get his job. Of course, it didn't happen, did it? The bloke went on a lot longer in the job than he was supposed to do. In the end I did nothing for about six or seven months and was losing lots of money at the time. I got the job in the end and I stayed with them for three years in their sales department. I had lots of freedom and a company car. I used to take clients out to dinner. It was an excellent job and I enjoyed it very much. I had a great boss to work for, which was helpful. Then they were taken over and all the sales force, from the managing director down, were made redundant.

I then got another sales job fairly quickly. It was with an engineering company. Again I had a company car, telephone and expenses. By this time, I had been in sales for about seven years and I was absolutely fed up with it. The driving got to me. Up and down the M25 and the M1. It was awful. I could see road rage looming. I was getting that way myself. Telling people where to go, honking the horn every five minutes and racing to get to appointments. I jacked that sort of life in about three years ago and apart from the odd job here and there, I don't do that much at all. My wife works full time, thankfully. I suppose you could call me a 'house husband'!

Jimmy still comes to Liverpool to see a few old friends and drop in at Goodison to watch the odd match, but his heart still lies in Newcastle. His family all still live in the Newcastle area and he often goes back home to see them. Geordies are said to be very much like Scousers, in terms of humour and passion for their respective cities and football. It's obvious that Jimmy has all these qualities. Of course he would have loved to have played for Newcastle United, but Everton got to him first and saw the best of his career. In fact when we asked him if he would have liked to have played for his home team he told us this story.

To be honest, without me sounding big-headed, Newcastle couldn't have afforded me. I remember putting that transfer request in when Alan Whittle had got my place in the team. The chief coach in those days was Wilf Dixon. He called me into his office and asked me why I was putting in a transfer request. He said, 'I know Alan has got your place at the moment, but you have to work hard to win it back and be patient.' I said that I wanted to play football in the first team and I didn't think that I would get my place back on a regular basis. He actually said to me then, 'Well, how many clubs in the country do you think can afford you?' I said I didn't know. He then said, 'Well, I'll tell you. It would be about four. Arsenal, Tottenham,

Liverpool and Manchester United. They'll be the only teams that could afford what we would ask for you. Do you think that you would be an automatic choice in those teams as well? These days it is a squad game.' I think Newcastle would have liked me to join them but to be truthful, I don't think they could have afforded me.

Jimmy still loves the game and is impressed with the quality of the Premiership. He thinks that it is good that foreign players have injected new ideas, even though he reckons that there could be friction between foreign and home-grown players. He looks back to his playing career with affection, especially the times he was an Everton player.

I think I was in one of the better eras for football. There were a greater number of characters in my day and at the start of the season you could point to at least ten teams that could win the league. Nowadays, you could probably say three, with confidence, will go on to win the Premiership. It seemed to be a lot harder in those days to play well week in week out. For example, I didn't like playing against Liverpool. I could never play my best against them. I don't know why it was like it was against them, but even with the likes of Gerry Byrne and Tommy Smith, who were not the quickest of players, I couldn't turn it on for the fans. I thought I played well against Leeds United. The strange thing about them was, I just got the feeling that they must have all gone to bed together as they were so close as a squad. One of the best players I played against was Bertie Vogts who played for Borussia Moenchengladbach. I remember that I had to play at my best just to keep up with him, which I felt I did in that European Cup match at Goodison in 1971. Really, playing in those days was a privilege because there were so many great players around in nearly every team.

Fame was not the same in the days when Jimmy was one of the Goodison heroes. An unusual way that Jimmy has been immortalised is that his name is featured in a recent film based on an idea from a book by Nick Hornby called *Fever Pitch*. In it there is a scene where cigarette cards are being swapped, when one character is trying to get rid of one of his two Jimmy Husband cards for another player. As Jimmy says, 'Fame at last.'

In our eyes, Jimmy was one of the true greats of Everton. He was exciting, could score goals and was genuinely a nice guy in a sport where usually you had to be very hard-faced to succeed. It's not difficult to understand why, in the school playgrounds in the late '60s, boys would often pretend to be Jimmy Husband.

CHAPTER TEN

Howard Kendall

EVERTON PLAYING CAREER: 1967–1974 AND 1981
GAMES PLAYED: 274
GOALS SCORED: 29
EVERTON MANAGERIAL CAREER: 1981–1987, 1990–1993, 1997–1998

If ever a footballer was in love with a club, then Howard Kendall was the man and Everton was the club. It seems like fate that Howard, at the time of writing this book, has returned to the club he joined as a 20 year old. Once again the most successful manager in Everton's history has taken the responsibility for making Everton a top-class club. Typically, he is modest about his achievements in the game, preferring to give the praise to all who worked around him. Howard was and still is a team man. He joined Everton in March 1967 as Harry Catterick was building one of the greatest midfield trios of all time in the history of the English game. Along with Colin Harvey and Alan Ball, Howard would thrill the knowledgeable Everton fans with the type of football that made Everton one of the teams of the 1960s. As soon as he joined the club he fell in love with it.

I moved to Everton just before my 21st birthday for £85,000. What had happened was that Frank McLintock had moved from Leicester City to Arsenal for that price, and Preston insisted that Everton pay the same amount, which was a record for a wing-half. The thing that struck me was the size of the place. Walking into Bellefield was very impressive. The facilities were second to none, and still are. The club was massive. At the time there were lots of newspaper reports about me going to Liverpool, but I think that at the time Preston thought there were too many players going from Preston to Liverpool. They, of course, didn't want to be seen as a nursery club. Really, I wanted to play for a big club in the then first division and Everton came in for me at the last minute. Mind you, Tottenham had shown interest along with Stoke City who made a last-ditch effort because, back then, clubs like Stoke were able to pay the transfer fee on hire purchase. The likes of Everton and other big clubs were monopolising the market in those days because they were able to pay cash. It was only through the hire purchase system that everybody had an equal chance of getting players.

Howard settled in at Everton and quickly established himself in the team. In the early years Howard was a little in awe of the players around him. After all, here was a player who, at the age of 17, had played at Wembley in an FA Cup final (in 1964) as the youngest-ever player to do so, and was now surrounded by some of the all-time greats of British football.

There were many characters in that dressing-room – Gordon West, Brian Labone and when I joined the club Alex Young was still there. Whenever it was mentioned about record fees and playing in an FA Cup final at 17, you were quickly brought down to earth as you looked around the dressing-room and saw the players who were established internationals, and other great players.

By now the midfield trio of Ball, Harvey and Kendall was being talked about by the fans as something a bit special, but Howard is quick to point out that really the midfielders won particular praise only because that was where the game was usually won or lost.

The great thing about that era was that it was a team effort. It wasn't down to individuals. Harry Catterick was a tremendous manager. His buying was excellent not because he bought me, but because he was good at getting the balance right. The thing about the three of us was that we gelled. We complemented each other and we got to know each other's style of play.

In 1968, Everton were back at Wembley for another FA Cup final, this time against West Bromwich Albion. In March of that year Everton had beaten them 6–2 at the Hawthorns and were easily the favourites to repeat their triumph of a couple of years before. So it was a massive shock when West Brom won the cup through a Jeff Astle goal.

Everyone was expecting a victory. We were odds-on favourites. We had beaten them by a large margin a few months previously so the favouritism was justified, but football has a funny habit of creating upsets. We were naturally very upset in the dressing-room after that game.

However, Everton were not down for too long. Two seasons later they were back on top as champions.

After that final in 1968 there was a determination amongst the players. I think that in the two seasons that followed, we played some of the best football ever. It was fantastic to play in such a team and we fully deserved to be champions in 1970.

The years that followed that championship year were a disappointment for Everton fans. After all, Everton were seen as the team of the '70s. Apart from an FA Cup semi-final against Liverpool at Old Trafford where Everton lost 2–1, they found it hard to scale the heights in the league that they had comprehensively achieved in 1970.

That was very disappointing but it's always a danger to be given a label. I remember Crystal Palace being mentioned as the team of the '80s. They were relegated in 1981. I think there were several reasons as to why we didn't capitalise on the success. There were players with injuries, players retiring and leaving. I don't think it was easy to replace players of the quality of Johnny Morrissey, Ray Wilson, Brian Labone and Alan Ball, and certainly not all at once.

Billy Bingham became manager in May 1973. In February 1974 Howard joined Birmingham City, along with defender Archie Styles, in a transfer deal which saw centre-forward Bob Latchford arrive at Goodison Park.

That was very disappointing for me. It came as a shock as well. Billy Bingham came in and wanted to make changes. I'd had two or three good years while the team had struggled and I'd won personal awards not just on Merseyside but nationally as well. He wanted to stamp his authority at Goodison and was probably thinking, 'Well, he goes and I'll bring in my own team.' No offence to Bob Latchford, Bob was a tremendous signing, but the disappointment to me was that Billy did not go out and buy Bob so that I could play with him. But I had a job to do which was to keep Birmingham in the first division, which we did on the last day of the season, which I suppose was against the odds, so in many respects the deal worked out well for Birmingham. I worked alongside another great player, Trevor Francis. I thought he was a tremendous player.

Howard stayed at Birmingham for two and a half years. There was a very different management style to what he had been used to at Everton. Freddie Goodwin took him into his confidence whereas Harry Catterick was seen as distant. Howard was made team captain and Freddie involved Howard in decision-making when it came to team matters, whereas at Everton, he didn't think that would have happened.

The confidence shown by Freddie in me helped me to concentrate on getting qualified as a coach. I had always wanted to stay in football. I didn't know in what capacity, but I knew I wanted to be involved as it was the only thing I had ever done.

In 1977, Howard joined Stoke City. This time his manager was an idol of his, George Eastham.

I used to watch George play for Newcastle and here I was working for him at Stoke. He was a tremendous influence on me. It was a fresh start for me after my time at Birmingham. Unfortunately George lost his job in the first season I was there. Alan Durban came in and appointed me player-coach. That gave me an insight to the backroom side of football and the involvement of being a manager or a coach, and what was needed to become one. The time consumed is a total shock to players going into management immediately they end their playing careers. So for me that was superb grounding. I virtually worked as an assistant manager to Alan Durban. We then won promotion to the then first division in my second season at Stoke. Alan thought that I might not be up to it in terms of carrying on playing at that level, I didn't agree with him on that and Blackburn then came in for me and offered me the player-manager's job at Ewood Park. They had just been relegated from the old division two to division three. I thought that that was a big enough club to make a really good push to come back up again.

Blackburn didn't have a lot of money in those days. There were board meetings about all sorts of things, including how many second-class stamps were to be bought. It was very tight there. Blackburn got promotion in the first year and then we were battling for promotion again the following season.

By now, Howard was beginning to make a very strong impression on chairmen of the bigger clubs, and before long Everton made an approach to get what would turn out to be the most successful manager in Everton's history.

In those days there was a general agreement amongst clubs that no manager would be poached during the season, but the Blackburn chairman was very annoyed when Everton made contact before the end of the season. At the time, obviously Everton were on my mind, but I wanted to finish the season with Blackburn being successful. On the last day of that season we won at Bristol Rovers but, unfortunately, Swansea had won at Preston, which meant that they were promoted on goal difference. At that time, in the back of my mind, I knew that I was going to Everton whether we had won promotion or not. It was similar to last season at Sheffield United. I would have loved it had Blackburn been a first division side, as I would have loved Sheffield United to have become a Premiership side this season. In the end there could have been only one decision I would have made and that was to come to Everton.

Now back on familiar territory, Howard had a tough job to do. Everton at that time were in a slump. The lure of Everton was overpowering for Howard. He has always loved the club.

The fans are really special. You know what Everton means to them. The size of the club is also a big factor. I mean I've got a great affection for Preston North End, Stoke City and wherever I've been, but you don't spend 17 years at one place as a player and manager without it being something special.

Putting Everton back on top was always going to be a hard task. Howard quickly brought in players to try and find the right blend and, more importantly, bring balance to the side.

I think it's well documented that I did try and sign a big-name player at that time. I went in for Bryan Robson and West Bromwich wouldn't sell him, and I tried to balance up the squad. We had something like five centre-backs and two midfielders, no wide players, and I just wanted to get the balance right first. They had finished 15th in the season before I arrived and in my first season they finished 8th. People talk about the magnificent seven, but they all weren't going to be successful but they were going to get us back on the road again. I even kept my player registration and I ended up playing four times in the first team. I didn't want to play, the idea was to play in the reserves, only to help the youngsters really. I enjoyed my player-management days. What I learnt was that when you're out there with them, and when they got used to the boss being out on the pitch, I could be of benefit to them. The youngsters then were no problem. You get to know which of them are good professionals in a short space of time. I think what happened at Blackburn was that when things were going wrong on the pitch, the players would turn round and look at me as if to say 'Well go on then, you're the boss, put it right,' and I had to get it over to them that if I was out there with them, I would try and put it right, but I was only one of the team.

Things began to go horribly wrong on the pitch in the first half of the 1983–84 season. By Christmas, some Everton fans wanted the board to take strong action by giving Howard the sack. The board of directors were having none of it and gave their support to Howard.

Well, I think that people knew that we were on the right lines. Both myself and the squad knew we were on the right lines, and that there was very little wrong with things. Whether or not one game going either way meant that I stayed or went, I don't know. A lot of people talk about that, but I was in my third season. Things had improved, but not in the way people had possibly wanted. At the start of that season we were not scoring goals, winning at home; gates were dropping and at a big club you do expect that sort of criticism or pressure on you.

Daily we were working with quality players, but unfortunately you need certain characters that when things are going wrong on the pitch and you have crowds of 13,000 getting angry at what they are watching, you need players who will stand up and be counted. I don't think there was a turning point in terms of a particular match, I was lucky enough to bring in two characters who had had injury problems and that we took a chance on [Andy Gray and Peter Reid]. They worked out to be the ingredient that we needed at the time. The players responded by showing the ability that I knew they had, with the likes of Gary Stevens and Peter Reid going on to become England international players because of the confidence they now had.

By the end of the 1983–84 season, Everton were involved in two cup finals – the Milk League Cup and the FA Cup. This was a remarkable turnaround in Everton's fortunes considering the way the season had looked to be heading. The Milk League Cup final was a very special occasion as the Blues' opponents were none other than Liverpool. This was the first time that the two Merseyside clubs had appeared in a final at Wembley. It was dubbed the 'friendly final', because the unique relationship between both sets of fans ensured that supporters of both teams could be seen standing side by side. Like most derby matches there was controversy. Everton were seen to be the victims of a dubious refereeing decision and the game ended up in stalemate at 0–0.

> We deserved to be at Wembley in both competitions. Of course for Everton fans it was a bit more special in the fact that Everton fans had had Liverpool rammed down their necks for quite a while. The Milk Cup draw at Wembley was hard on us really. Everybody in the ground saw that we should have had a penalty when Alan Hansen handled in the box. To come away with a draw, though, we showed that we more than held them. The team gave our supporters the respect in the city that they had not had in a while. Even though we lost the replay at Maine Road, the fans had something else to look forward to by going back to Wembley in the FA Cup final against Watford. The players were determined to go again. Andy Gray had been cup-tied in the other competition and he was determined to go to Wembley. That was a great occasion. It was the first time that the club had won a trophy for 14 years. The fans then started to think about being in European competition, so the atmosphere at that time was extremely good. That was just the beginning as far as I was concerned. After all, you know you are deemed to have 'arrived' when you win the Championship, as then you can say that we were the best in England. The balance of the side was superb and our football style was akin to the sort of football that people remembered from the days of Harry Catterick.

Everton went on to win just about everything in the 1984–85 season. They won the League Championship, the reserve-team league, the Youth Cup final, that season's Charity Shield again against Liverpool and, of course, the European Cup Winners' Cup, which was the club's first European trophy. Accounts of that game are contained elsewhere in this book. The following season saw Everton finish strongly and again go to Wembley for the FA Cup final. As far as Blues' fans were concerned, this was getting to be like a permanent fixture. Again the opposition was Liverpool. This time Liverpool won 3–1. The season's top scorer was Gary Lineker, but even he could not prevent Liverpool winning. But as Howard pointed out he would rather the club had got to Wembley than have been defeated in the semi-final. The following season saw Everton win the Championship again. However the lure of Spain proved to be very tempting. Frustrated by English clubs not being allowed to play in European competitions, Howard wanted to test his managerial skills with a European club. Atletico Bilbao was the club that secured his services.

> The ban in Europe was a tremendous blow to Everton Football club and the supporters, football-wise. I had had an offer from Barcelona before I eventually joined Bilbao. Terry Venables had decided to stay at Barcelona and I had stayed with Everton and won the League again in 1987. But really I had always had the idea of managing a European club and I had to get it out of my system. The people from Bilbao came over and sold me on the idea of managing them. It was a great experience. They are situated in the north so it wasn't too hot. I found the language difficult to overcome at first and I had an interpreter, but in the end you've got to work hard to get to grips with such things. I lived with a Spanish family, which helped me a lot. In my first year we got into the UEFA Cup competition after being in the relegation play-offs the season before I joined. It was an achievement to get into European competition with an all-Basque team. They were all good players over there and I was pleased to be working with excellent players. They live for football there. I was there for two and half years and then the president of the club was up for re-election and we came to an agreement that I would also go, as he felt that he was not going to get re-elected if we didn't qualify for Europe. We were not having the best of times when I left. We had lost three games on the trot and there was speculation about my future anyway. It was considered a long time for a foreign coach at that time, and I had made up my mind to come back to England.

Because he still lived in the north-west, Howard was hoping that, having left England as a manager of a championship team, he would be offered one of the bigger clubs to manage. Manchester City were the one big club that seemed to be in decline and, as one of the top north-west clubs, offered the chance that Howard was hoping for.

Manchester City were heading for relegation but once again Howard managed to draw on his vast experience in guiding them just away from the drop zone. He brought in players whom he had worked with at Everton, as he felt again that the side needed to get the balance right. Those ex-Everton players helped enormously, as he knew their strengths and weaknesses very well. He sold players and sometimes this was not popular with the fans. When, however, they saw that results were going for them because Howard had got the balance right, most people backed him to the hilt. A lot has been made of the selling of Andy Hinchcliffe to Everton, but in truth Howard felt that he wanted a goalkeeper. Everton wanted Hinchcliffe. The deal was that Everton would give Neil Pointon plus-£600,000 in exchange for him. This meant that Tony Coton was brought in as the new City goalkeeper. Once again getting the balance right was all that mattered if Manchester City were to survive as a top club.

Soon Everton seemed to be going through a crisis period of their own. Colin Harvey had taken over as manager when Howard left for Spain. Things had not worked out for Colin, apart from getting to Wembley in 1989. The following season saw Everton slipping further, and in October 1990 Colin was relieved of his duties. Nobody would have believed that the next manager would be Howard. In fact he was very surprised that Everton approached him just a few days after Colin had been asked to step down. However, in November 1990, Howard came back to the club that had seen so much success when he was last there as manager. Not only had Howard come back, but his assistant was none other than Colin Harvey. The two of them certainly had a big job on their hands in ensuring that Everton did not become the whipping boys of the top division. By the end of the season Everton had finished ninth. The rest of Howard's spell was not so productive. It soon became clear that the club was facing an even bigger struggle.

Everton were the subject of a boardroom battle for control over the club. Howard was caught in the middle from the very beginning of this struggle. He had shown interest in Manchester United's striker Dion Dublin. The board at that time refused to sanction the deal, which left Howard in an untenable position. Faced with the prospect that his club was going downhill rapidly off the pitch, even though Everton were in a respectable position on it, Howard knew that if the board wouldn't back his judgement, there would be no point in staying. So in October 1993 Howard resigned, after Everton had beaten Southampton at Goodison.

He then went to Greece as manager of Xanthi, and in 1994 he was offered the chance to move back into management in England with Notts. County, who were in the first division (the old second division). Things did not turn out in the way Howard would have liked and Howard was sacked after less than a year. In 1995 he joined Sheffield United, who were also a team struggling in the first division. In a season and a half he turned them around. By the end of the 1996–97 season Sheffield came within minutes of securing their place in the Premiership via the play-offs when they were beaten 1–0 by Crystal Palace.

While we were writing this book, Everton were looking for a new manager after Joe Royle left the club in March 1997. Howard's name was eventually linked with the club that he obviously loves more than anywhere else and he is now manager again. The marriage has taken on a new lease of life. Long may it reign.

CHAPTER ELEVEN

Roger Kenyon

EVERTON PLAYING CAREER: 1964–1979
GAMES PLAYED: 305
GOALS SCORED: 9

Tall, brave and strong, yet also remarkably adept on the ball, Roger Kenyon never achieved the enormous success he seemed destined for when he first burst onto the scene at Goodison in the late '60s.

At Everton, the bustling, bristling centre-back found his opportunities limited in the early days by the colossus figure of club captain Brian Labone. And when he did finally establish himself in the '70s, ironically it was during a period of considerable under-achievement for the Blues. And at international level, despite confident predictions that he was an England centre-half in the making in his younger days, Kenyon came up against Derby's Roy McFarland, a truly world-class defender. Frustratingly, Kenyon only ever got as far as the England substitutes' bench, never actually taking those few extra paces which would have at least earned him the full cap that his talents clearly deserved.

Yet, Kenyon spent nearly 15 years at Everton, becoming the epitome of the loyal servant, when many lesser players would have slapped in a transfer request.

Born in Blackpool, the young Roger made steady progress towards the very top, playing for the England Schoolboys. He was widely admired and courted by a number of top clubs, before inking a deal with Everton.

Everton showed more interest in me than anyone else. And to be honest they also had a better set-up for young players than any other club I saw, so I was quite happy to sign on for them. I went straight from school to Goodison in 1964 at the age of 15, and at first I have to admit I was overawed by the place. Anybody my age would have been. It was just an awesome club. Everything about it was huge. I'd been used to being something of a big fish in a little pond. I was king of the hill as a schoolboy player. Suddenly I was a nothing, and had to start right at the bottom.

Like all apprentices in those days, I did a lot of menial jobs at the club. I cleaned the first-team players' boots, washed out the toilets, things like that. I know these days coaches decry that sort of thing, believing that youngsters join clubs to play football and should do just that rather than being used as cheap labour, but one thing I did learn from doing all of that was a sense of discipline. It also knocked any arrogance I might have had right out of me. You quickly get a sense of proportion, which I think is important. And watching the first-team players leaving after training in their nice cars made me hungry to be one of them.

Kenyon got his big chance in the first team in 1968, and he grabbed it with both hands, even if he did have an initial attack of nerves.

My début was against Burnley at Turf Moor, and we drew 1–1. In those days, Burnley were a good top-flight side. They were packed with big names, and having to face up to a centre forward like the Scot Andy Lochhead, who was big, strong and highly experienced, was very nerve-wracking I can tell you. I was almost panicking with a sort of stage fright before going out on the pitch. I suppose it happens to every young player when they make their first-team début. It's a dream that you so desperately do not want to turn into a nightmare. But Brian Labone, who was of course captain at the time and my centre-back partner for the game, was brilliant. He calmed me down and told me that if Harry Catterick didn't think I was any good, then he wouldn't have picked me. Brian said I was in the side because I could do the job, no more, no less. When someone of Brian's reputation and stature takes the time and trouble to talk to you like that, it does make a big difference.

The first 15 or 20 minutes were nervy for me, but once I got in a few tackles and won the ball, it all just seemed to flow naturally and I settled into the side.

In the late '60s opportunities for Kenyon were few and far between, but he did get the chance to play a part in Everton's ride to Wembley and the FA Cup final in '68.

John Hurst, who was Brian's regular centre-back partner, went down with jaundice before the quarter-final against Leicester, which let me in. And we beat them 3–1 that day, at Filbert Street.

And I also stayed there for the semi-final when we beat Leeds 1–0 at Old Trafford, thanks to a Johnny Morrissey penalty. That is such a great memory. We were definitely the underdogs that day, and to beat the mighty Leeds – what a moment to savour.

However, at Wembley itself, against West Bromwich Albion, Kenyon was the substitute, with Hurst back in the team.

I was really pleased to be involved in some capacity with the final, because it's such a special occasion, and so many players just never get even close, but I would have loved to be on the pitch and actually involved. Mind you, every time one of our lot went down with an injury, I was praying that they'd get back up again, because the butterflies would start up and there was a slight fear of actually having to go out there and perform in front of 100,000 people, plus the millions watching on TV around the world. Still, it never happened anyway.

Everton, of course, lost 1–0 to an extra-time goal, and Kenyon recalls the aftermath with a sense of sadness, even after all these years.

We were the hot favourites to win the cup. We'd beaten Albion in both league games that season, and certainly should have buried them in the final. We had the chances, but just couldn't score, and we were made to suffer in extra time when Jeff Astle scored what proved to be the winner. In footballing terms, that was the saddest day of my life. We sloped off the pitch at the end with our heads down and our losers' medals. In the dressing-room afterwards, there were lads actually crying. We were desperately upset at having let ourselves and fans down. True, we did thrash West Bromwich Albion 4–0 very early on the following season, but even that never made up for what happened at Wembley. And, as it turned out, I never got another chance to put things right in an FA Cup final.

But in 1969–70, Kenyon did get the chance to play a vital role in helping to steer Everton through the home straight to the championship, replacing the injured Labone on the run-in, and his mature performances helped steady the nerves as the finishing line came into view. But, unfortunately, he didn't play in enough games that season to actually qualify for a championship medal! And, soon after, of course, the team began to break up, for one reason or another. Kenyon still has difficulty in understanding exactly what happened, and coming to terms with it.

Every now and then I take out scrapbooks from that period and look at the players we had, how young so many of us were, and wonder what went wrong. By rights we should have dominated football for several years. Look at the names: West, Wright, Newton, Kendall, Labone, Harvey, Husband, Ball, Royal, Hurst, Morrissey, Jackson, Whittle. Sure, a few of them were coming towards the end of their careers, but a lot of those players were still a few years short of their peak. We had a sparkling future. Or at least we should have had one. But it didn't work out that way.

Harry sold off Alan Ball to Arsenal in 1971, because he believed he'd got the best years out of him and it was time to offload Ball. What a mistake that was! Alan enjoyed several more years at the top, and he could have been a crucial part of the Everton set-up for years. That transfer was the catalyst for everything that happened. The whole thing seemed to fall apart. It was a huge mistake to sell him.

Kenyon has considerable respect for Catterick, even though it's tinged with a certain clear-eyed cynicism.

Harry was obviously a good manager, but he was very difficult to get along with. He ruled the club with a rod of iron. You could never say no to the man, and I was taught that from the age of 15 when I joined the club. Some of the senior players did find him hard to take, but that was the way he was, a disciplinarian but also someone who knew what he was doing.

But you did sometimes wonder whether he would deliberately duck confrontations. I remember when I was a very young player, Fred Pickering was one of the big stars at the club. Anyway, one day Harry decided that Fred was overweight and had to come back in the afternoon for extra training. So, Harry told the first-team trainer, who told the reserve-team trainer, who told the youth-team trainer, who told me to go and interrupt Fred's lunch and tell him the bad news.

Talk about passing the buck. You can imagine how I felt. Here I was, just a kid, being ordered to go and tell an England international star that he must come back for extra training. It was very unfair, but I had no choice. So I went up to Pickering and, as politely as I could, told him Catterick's instructions. Fred was furious, as you can imagine. But by the time I'd told Fred, the manager had gone home! He was nowhere to be found. He'd just avoided an argument with one of his top players. But Fred was back doing the training. He had little choice. In those days, managers were all-powerful. They could virtually make a player do anything they wished. Of course, now the boot's on the other foot and it's the players who have the whip hand.

But whilst Kenyon has a degree of respect for Catterick, he found his successor Billy Bingham a little hard to stomach.

Harry certainly believed in fitness, but Billy Bingham was far worse. He carried it to extremes. It was ridiculous. Every Monday morning, for instance, we were expected to run 3,000 metres in 12 minutes – and Monday was the easy day in the training regime. He got us totally knackered, and then put us up against the reserves in a match. It was just crazy. I know people have this view of Bingham as a happy-go-lucky Irishman who loved attractive football, but that wasn't really the case at all.

The Bingham years were frustrating for Kenyon, who not so long before had been part of one of the finest teams in English club history.

Everton spent money left, right and centre, but some of the players Billy brought in were clearly not up to the job. They were over-priced. I can tell you, those years were really annoying and irritating. We just didn't seem to be going anywhere.

When Bingham was replaced by Gordon Lee, things did pick up a little. Certainly Kenyon's opinion of Lee is far higher than that of Bingham.

Gordon was totally different to Billy. I got on all right with him. He was an honest, hard-working fella who wanted the players to give 100 per cent, and he also believed in playing good football. Gordon came so close to winning things for Everton. I just think he lacked the element of luck all teams need to win trophies. We would get so near, and then something would go wrong – a referee's decision, a bad injury at a crucial time. It was as if he was destined never to win anything, which was such a shame.

Under Lee, Everton of course reached the League Cup final at Wembley in 1977. But this wasn't to provide any consolation for Kenyon for the failure in 1968. After three games, the Blues lost to Aston Villa. He says: 'That wasn't exactly a high spot of my career. In the first replay I actually managed to put the ball in my own goal. Great!'

And towards the end of his time at Everton, Kenyon was struck with several injuries, particularly hamstring problems, which meant he was in and out of the side.

It was an awful period for me. I just didn't seem to be able to shake off my injury problems. Then at the start of the 1978–79 season I played against Arsenal, and went in to tackle Malcolm MacDonald, and would you believe my luck? He fell right on top of me and my knee ligaments just went. As a result I was out eight weeks, and that really marked the end of my Everton career.

Surprisingly, Kenyon left Everton and moved to Canada. He joined the Vancouver Whitecaps in 1979.

I actually hadn't planned to leave the club, but then I met John Craven, whom I knew from Blackpool, and he suggested that I consider a move abroad to Canada. Now, at the time Tony Waiters was managing the team, and he was yet another connection with Blackpool [Waiters played in goal for Blackpool and England during the '60s], so I agreed to go out and talk to him, and he sold me on the idea of joining the Whitecaps. And there was certainly no lack of English players already out there. Alan Ball played for them, so did the old Derby striker Kevin Hector, Trevor Wymark [ex-Ipswich], and Willie Johnston [who was once a top name with Glasgow Rangers]. And Bruce Grobbelaar was our goalkeeper before he came to England to join Liverpool.

Bob McNab, the Arsenal full-back, was the coach in Vancouver, and I got on really well with him. In fact, I owe Bob a lot. I'd had so many problems with hamstring injuries, and despite seeing several specialists, nothing seemed to work. Bob told me that he'd had a similar problem and had been cured by acupuncture. Well, with nothing to lose I went and saw an acupuncturist – and it worked. I was sorted out in no time. I just wish someone had told me about acupuncture earlier on in my career.

And, finally, at the Whitecaps Kenyon got a winners' medal.

In my first season out there, we beat the New York Cosmos in the cup final. It was a real feather in our cap because the Cosmos were really the team of the stars. They had Pelé and Beckenbauer, legends like that. So to win the cup was a huge triumph for us. And it was nice to collect a winners' medal, even if it was in the North American Soccer League.

Kenyon did briefly return to English football, but only as a way of keeping fit during the North American close season.

Tony Waiters came up with the idea of placing some of the players with English clubs during the close season. He felt it would keep us fit and help with the next season in North America. I joined up with Bristol City and trained with them. I didn't actually join them, but I did turn out four times in the first team, and it certainly kept me fighting fit.

In 1980, Kenyon finally quit playing, but had no plans to stay in the game.

Well, I had been in football since I was 15, but to be honest I'd had enough. I just had no interest in getting into coaching or management. So I tried various business ventures, including a fruit and veg shop, before getting into the pub game. I worked at it for 12 years, before giving it up. Nowadays, I'm on the after-dinner circuit, which is very lucrative for so many ex-players. I don't get involved with the posh, bow-tie dinners, but more the informal ones. And I really enjoy it.

Sadly, Kenyon makes few trips back to Goodison, where he would be sure of a hero's welcome every time.

You know, I would like to be asked to do the half-time raffle draw on the pitch. That would be nice. Maybe someone will read this and actually invite me along to do it. That would be a thrill, to walk out at Goodison onto the pitch after all these years. Yes, they're still a special club to me, even though I don't get there very often.

In a career that was distinguished, but sadly lacking in tangible footballing rewards (there are few medals for him to polish), one of Kenyon's biggest regrets is that he never got a full England cap.

When Don Revie was manager of England I was picked for the squad a total of six times, and each time I ended up on the subs' bench just kicking my heels. Don kept promising me that he'd put me in the side, but he never did. You know, I really just wish that he'd allowed me to get on to the pitch for just a few minutes, because that would have qualified me for a full cap, which would have been a lovely moment and something to really cherish. But it wasn't to be, and I suppose I'm lucky to have been considered good enough to be picked for a squad in the first place.

Who knows, perhaps if Everton had been more successful in the '70s then I'd have picked up some caps and even won a few more medals, but you can't run your life on what might have been, and I'm grateful that I was able to play for such a great club as Everton, and to have been involved in the 1970 championship-winning side.

That's Roger Kenyon – a man whose qualities both as a professional player and as person might never have been rewarded as they should have been, but who still looks on the bright side of his life.

CHAPTER TWELVE

Brian Labone

EVERTON PLAYING CAREER: 1958–1971
GAMES PLAYED: 530
GOALS SCORED: 2

There is no more passionate or committed Evertonian than Brian Labone. In fact, it's probably only a cruel twist of fate that prevents Labone from having a blue and white skin. But what does it matter? Labone wears his heart very much on his sleeve, and his veins course with 'Blue' blood.

'My first trip to Goodison Park came when I was just nine or ten years old. My father took me to see my first game, and from then on I stood regularly in the boys' pen at the Gwladys Street End,' recalls Labone.

In July 1957, at the tender age of 17, the tall young central-defender signed for the club, giving up a possible university place to concentrate on what would be a distinguished football career. And progress was rapid.

I made my début in 1958 at St Andrews against Birmingham City, replacing the great Tommy [T.E.] Jones at centre-half. Unfortunately, we lost 2–1. And we didn't do much better on my home début, losing 4–3 to Spurs. Tottenham's centre-forward that day, Bobby Smith, gave me the right run-around and three of the goals I have to admit were down to me. So I was banished back to the reserves for the rest of the season!

But Labone didn't have long to wait before establishing himself in the first team, under the management of Johnny Carey. And by the time Harry Catterick took over as Everton's manager in 1961, he was an integral part of the team.

Indeed, such was his rapid progress that the classy centre-half made his England début in 1962, amazingly becoming the first Everton player to appear for England since the Second World War – a great honour.

> I made my début in a home international against Wales, marking none other than Roy Vernon, whom I knew really well because he was one of Everton's top players! Was I nervous about playing for England? Not really. I was used to playing in front of big crowds in the first division, and I also knew most of the Welsh players from league matches. But it was still amazing progress for me. Here I was, someone who nearly gave up a football career to go to university, and just a few years later I was representing my country!

Labone's international career was slightly chequered. He earned 26 caps in eight years, part of the reason for this rather poor return being his amazing decision in 1966 to withdraw from contention for inclusion in England's World Cup squad to concentrate on his marriage plans. But he did appear in the finals of the World Cup in Mexico four years later, having supplanted '66 hero Jack Charlton at the heart of the defence. Sadly, most people will recall that tournament for the fact that England managed to let slip a two-goal lead against West Germany in the quarter-finals, losing 3–2 after extra time, although the elegant Labone wasn't to blame for any of the German goals.

Back at Everton, though, the consistent Labone was a cornerstone of the 1962–63 championship-winning side, and in 1964 he took over the captaincy from the disgraced Tony Kay (jailed for his part in a match-fixing ring when he was his previous club, Sheffield Wednesday), leading the club to an FA Cup triumph in 1966 and the league championship in 1969–70.

But Labone nearly missed the last success. In 1967 he publicly stated his intention of quitting the game 18 months hence.

> I was suffering from injury and loss of form at the time, and was planning to go into the family business. My father ran a central heating company called J. & B. Labone, and that's where my future lay – at least that's what I thought. But he died in 1969, and that changed everything. I ended up staying on at Everton for another couple of seasons.

Brian's change of heart delighted all Evertonians, because there was little doubt that his calm authority would have been badly missed. As it was, Labone suffered a major injury during the run-in to the championship success of 1970, forcing him to sit on the sidelines as Roger Kenyon took his place in the team, and Alan Ball assumed the captaincy.

Eventually, an Achilles tendon injury forced his retirement in 1971, at the comparatively early age of 31. But Labone shows no bitterness or resentment towards his bad luck in this respect. In fact, the man's enthusiasm for his years at Everton remains undimmed, especially when it comes to discussing one particular character at the club, goalkeeper Gordon West.

We had a lot of great characters there during the '60s, but Westie . . . Well, he was a one-off. We actually shared a room on away trips for ten years, and used to read stamp books in bed. Honestly! You might think the two of us would get up to all sorts of mischief, but we didn't at all.

I remember one particular game with Westie. It was in 1966 at St James' Park, against Newcastle United. Now Gordon had a huge throw-out. He could throw the ball two-thirds of the pitch. So every time he got the ball, I would turn away expecting to see the ball fly over my head from one of his throws. Now, on this night, Newcastle had an inside-forward called Albert Bennett, who buzzed around all game annoying Westie. Anyway, Westie threw the ball over the halfway line about 30 times during the game, so when he got the ball again towards the end of the match I turned away as usual, expecting to see it fly over my head. But it never did. I looked back into our area to see Gordon holding his hip and Albert lying flat out! It didn't take much to figure out what had happened. Gordon got sent off, and our Scottish defender, Sandy Brown, went in goal.

Now Sandy was Gordon's patsy. He loved taking the piss out of him. So Sandy went in goal and dived the wrong way for the penalty! You should have heard Gordon on the journey back home. He just had a constant go at poor old Sandy for going the wrong way!

On another occasion, we played Liverpool in an FA Cup fifth round game at Goodison in 1967. Everton stayed up in Blackpool for a couple of days before the big match. Now Gordon's wife had just given birth to a boy, so when we found out that there was a horse called West Boy running in a race it seemed like an omen. Moreover, the nearest betting shop to us in Blackpool was on West Street. And, of course, which club had Gordon played for before joining Everton? Blackpool. We were all convinced the horse was a cast-iron winner, so all of us put a tenner on West Boy.

Now, it should have come in first at 100–1 or something and made us all a fortune. Er, it didn't. The horse came third! Still, we won the cup tie, Alan Ball scoring at the Gwladys Street End.

Labone has a fund of such stories. A happy-go-lucky character, these days he uses his experiences to keep audiences enthralled as an after-dinner speaker. He also works on the public relations side at Goodison Park during match days and sits on the Spot The Ball panel for a local newspaper. But his main job is working in insurance.

> I suppose I've always been a bit of a drifter. I never had any real plans laid when I gave up football, so I've gone from job to job. Would I like to have gone into coaching or management? Maybe. But I never put out feelers in that direction. Still, I've had an interesting life. And football is so much more sophisticated these days than when I first started out. Under Ian Buchan, Everton had seven set formations for corners, numbered from one to seven. They were rotated in turn during a match. But we all got so confused that by the time we got a fourth corner, nobody could remember what we should be doing . . .

Brian Labone – an elegant, stylish defender. At his best world class. A man who still loves the game and the club who gave him the chance to play it. He says: 'I suppose I regard myself these days as someone who spreads the good word about Everton wherever and whenever I can.'

CHAPTER THIRTEEN

Bob Latchford

EVERTON PLAYING CAREER: 1974–1981
GAMES PLAYED: 289
GOALS SCORED: 138

When you think of all the players who have worn the number nine shirt, with all its traditions, you feel one of the greatest to wear it was Bob Latchford. Here was a man who terrified opponents. His awareness around the box was superb. His goal tally was tremendous. Goals were his business. He is still the third-highest goalscorer behind Graeme Sharp and, of course, Bill 'Dixie' Dean. Big and powerful, although not always the quickest, he could finish a match with goals that some of today's players just could not attempt.

He came to Goodison in a then record-breaking transfer of £350,000 with Howard Kendall and Archie Styles moving to Birmingham City in part exchange. As soon as he arrived he felt at home.

> I loved the facilities at the club. Everything was so big. It was a great feeling being part of such a set-up. I was made to feel very welcome and the club looked after the players. Billy Bingham was a good boss. He was tough and made us work very hard. I didn't particularly enjoy training but then I think we needed to work hard at it to bring out the best in us. When I arrived Everton were having a pretty good season and the team was fairly settled, but I soon got my chance. I made my début at West Ham. Unfortunately we lost 4–3. I scored my first a couple of weeks later at Leicester. Again we lost, but at least I had got on to the scoresheet.

Soon Bob was banging them in regularly and he finished his first season with 7 goals in 13 appearances. Of course, the fans took to him almost immediately. He had a good rapport with them and would often run straight to the fans whenever he scored. It wasn't long before he was recognised as the natural replacement for that other great 'number nine' Joe Royle.

There were some great players when I joined. Dave Lawson, Colin Harvey was still there and John Hurst. Great characters as well. I was aware that Everton had a tradition about the number nine shirt but I didn't think about it all that much. You just got on with the job. I was brought in to score goals which I did.

He certainly did do that. In his first four seasons he finished top league scorer for the team. Unfortunately, Everton were living under the shadow of Liverpool that was to haunt the club throughout the '70s.

Liverpool were always going one better than us throughout my time there. That was pretty awful because I have always believed that had we won a trophy in my time at Everton, we could have gone on to great things. It just wouldn't happen for us. We certainly had the talent and we came close on a number of occasions. The obvious time being the League Cup final against Aston Villa in 1977.

By then, Everton had that other great talent Duncan McKenzie alongside Bob. It was a treat to watch two very different players in style, who could guarantee excitement every time.

Yes, Duncan was the one-man show. Famous for his tricks and well-taken goals. We had a good team spirit in that season. Mick Lyons was a real character.
So was Terry Darracott and of course there was Andy King. But even with all those players we still couldn't pull off a trophy. The Aston Villa games were probably the hardest matches but I'll always remember the goals I scored, particularly the extra-time one at Hillsborough.

By now Billy Bingham had left the club and Gordon Lee was in charge. It was the 1977–78 season when Bob made his biggest impact at the club. It was the season he was to score 30 goals and to pocket a prize of £10,000 put up by a national newspaper.

At the start of the season I wasn't really taking much notice of the prize.

I don't think anybody was. But as the season went by I was beginning to think that I could be in with a chance. By the end of the year I had scored 19 goals and as long as I didn't pick up any bad injuries I thought I could do it. Then I went through a funny spell until March when the goals started to go in for me. The last match against Chelsea at home was a bit special. I had to score two more to get the prize. The crowd were willing me on. When we got a penalty I had no hesitation in taking it. Funnily enough in that season I took the only two penalties I have ever taken in my career. I suppose I never really counted penalties as goals. Maybe I should have done. Looking back now I might have scored another 20 or 30 goals in my career. But when that one went in against Chelsea it felt marvellous. It was a great achievement and I was proud that I had done it. In fact I think the reason the paper had put up the prize in the first place was because only one other person, Francis Lee, had scored 30 or above in one season throughout the decade. This was probably because in that decade you had the meanest defences that British football had ever known. The quality of those players was superb.

In 1977, Bob made his England début in a friendly against Italy. He was eventually capped 12 times for his country.

Funnily enough I don't remember too much about how it all came about in getting my first cap. All I remember was that it was against Italy at Wembley in 1977. I remember going up the tunnel and that it was nerve-wracking. The whole England set-up was vastly different from Everton. With England you are for all intents and purposes a stranger even though you know the other players. It was always a relaxed feeling being with them but it was still very different being a new boy. Kevin Keegan said to me that it would probably take about five or six games before I would feel part of the set-up. I was very proud to be part of the international team and I enjoyed it.

By now, Gordon Lee had settled into the managerial hot seat. Looking back at the Gordon Lee era today, some Everton fans seem to think that Gordon was not up to the mark when it came to getting the best from the players and that he didn't get the respect that managers deserve.

Gordon was very passionate about football. When you look back at his record it was not as bad as people today make out. The trouble was that Liverpool were going through their most successful period and were so dominating in the game that other teams, and especially us, were always going to struggle to get the recognition that we felt we deserved. As I've said had we won that League Cup final I believe that we would also have gone onto further success. It just shows how fine that dividing line is between failure and success. Gordon seemed to get a lot of stick because he didn't win a trophy, but we played some very good football as well at the time. When people look back we had two excellent seasons under Gordon when we finished third and then fourth. He managed to get the belief back into the team. He wasn't as aggressive as Billy but he was no less passionate in the way he wanted us to play football. He liked it played from the back through midfield. At the time we also had a very good coach in Steve Burtenshaw. The combination seemed to work. I always felt that we were one or two players short of having a championship team.

The 1980–81 season saw a slump in Everton's form, with them only just avoiding the drop into the old second division. By May Gordon Lee's reign was over and Howard Kendall became manager. Bob had moved on to Swansea City.

That was a bit of a culture shock for me. I think, looking back, I left Everton a bit too early, but I am one of those people who, having made a decision, will not go back on it and I had made that decision before Howard took over. I felt I couldn't go any further with Everton. By the time I left I had become the highest post-war goalscorer at the club. Not that I was conscious of it at the time. But I was very pleased to have got that record. I actually thought it would have been a lot higher maybe around 140 to 150 goals. I believe I am still in the top three.

Swansea was a bit of an up and down time for me. For two and a bit seasons I was happy, but then things started to go wrong on and off the pitch. We were relegated and the club was in a financial mess. Things fell apart quite dramatically. Mind you, I still scored 32 goals in the 1982–83 season.

Bob left troubled Swansea in 1984 and had a short spell in Holland with Breda. He was only there 6 months, but he still got 13 goals in 16 games.

That was a very interesting time in my football career. They played a very different type of formation at the time. They played with three men at the back, with two wing-backs, two wide players and somebody in the middle, and then I had two wingers and me up front. I had played with one winger at Everton. Dave Thomas would supply a lot of the balls for me, so I was quite used to the front line-up except I now had two supplying me. It's something that is now very much part of today's game. I had a good time there scoring 13 goals and we got promotion that year as well. Maybe I should have stayed at Breda, but I had an offer to come back to England to play for Coventry and, again, once I made the decision I stuck to it.

Bob only stayed at Coventry for a season. He didn't play that many games for them and was loaned out to Lincoln City. Towards the end of that season he went to Newport where he helped them stay in the third division.

Bob then moved on to Merthyr Tydfil where he helped them win the Welsh Cup and then play in Europe. It was a satisfying end to a remarkable career. He then drifted out of the game. At one time he would have liked to have gone into the coaching and management side but the opportunities never materialised. It has taken eight years to get involved in the game again. In 1995, Bob started working for Ladbrokes, the betting shop chain. He was once more in the public eye, often appearing on television. He has seen a dramatic change in football in the last five years.

Today's game is very different. Whether it is better for all the money and the hype, I don't know. It is very exciting but not necessarily better. For instance, Manchester United, for me, didn't play as well as they have done and yet they were still good enough to win the Premiership. I think Sky have now packaged, promoted and sold it very well. My only fear is where are the young players going to come from in Britain as there are so many foreign players being brought in who are not going to stay long term. In my day I remember the likes of Kevin Richardson, Steve McMahon and Graeme Sharp from Everton and Dean Saunders from when I was at Swansea all coming through the ranks. But it is getting less in terms of numbers coming from youth teams. I do, after all, have a vested interest now as I'm at Birmingham City looking after their youth policy. But I still think that we have enough home-grown talent that unfortunately can't make the breakthrough because foreign players have been brought in. There are one or two bigger clubs that do have an excellent youth policy and will maybe buy one or two foreign players but at least they are giving the younger ones the chance to make it. For instance, when I was in Holland I didn't notice too many foreign players, but what I did notice was their younger players were encouraged by their clubs. I remember one lad in particular playing for Feyenoord. He was big, strong and very skilful. Everybody knew he would make it in the game. It was Ruud Gullit. He wasn't the only one, though, because the Dutch knew that their kids would come through the system. Now that I'm at Birmingham I can hopefully bring a good number of our youth players through. I'm thoroughly enjoying it. Trevor Francis brought me in as I used to do some scouting for him when he was at Sheffield Wednesday. There is a lot of potential at Birmingham despite not having the same standard of facilities as at Goodison. I must admit that this would hopefully be the first step back on the road to management.

In talking to him, one learns that he is very knowledgeable about the game and how it should be played. As long as there's plenty of goals he would be happy. After all, goals were his trademark. He would surely rank as one of the best strikers that you would want in your team of all-time heroes of Goodison.

CHAPTER FOURTEEN

Duncan McKenzie

EVERTON PLAYING CAREER: 1976–1978
GAMES PLAYED: 62
GOALS SCORED: 21

If he hadn't been one of the 1970s' consummate footballing entertainers, Duncan McKenzie would probably have been on the stage, giving people the benefit of his showbiz personality, maybe as a conjuror making objects disappear right in front of your very eyes.

Flamboyant, exuberant, egotistical, inventive, eccentric, extrovert. All of these terms apply to McKenzie, a man equally at home trying to hurl a golf ball from one end of a football pitch to the other, nutmegging a defender, or trying to leap over a mini! Rarely has a footballer been blessed with such sublime skills and the temerity to use his genius on the most inappropriate of occasions. Duncan McKenzie lit up every club he graced, and none more so than Everton during the dark, grey days of the '70s.

I was only at Goodison for a couple of years, but everyone thinks I was there a lot longer. I go to London and fans there just think of me as an Evertonian. I go up to Sunderland and I get the same treatment. People just associate me more with Everton than any other club I played for, which is strange, but it says something about the way I was treated by the fans and the club. They are special to me.

McKenzie was part of an era when footballing extravagance was taken for granted, when the lure of multiple tactical complexities and the pressure of mega-money rewards were sublimated to the ideal of sport as escapism. Fans flocked to Goodison to watch McKenzie, never knowing whether they would see a god in full glorious flow, or an indifferent iconoclast.

Perhaps only Swede Anders Limpar has since come close to evincing the same feelings of fangloria and frustration at the club in recent years.

> You know, I love Scousers because they're so straightforward and honest with you. If I had a bad game, there would be none of this pussyfooting around from the fans. They'd just say, 'Duncan, we love you, but you had an absolute stinker today!' – or words to that effect!

It was his father-in-law's illness that led to the mercurial McKenzie joining Everton in November 1976 for a fee of £200,000.

> I was playing in Belgium at the time for Anderlecht. Now, my wife's from Liverpool, and when her father became ill she came back home. Sadly, he died from cancer, and we all went through a very difficult period, as you can imagine.
>
> My brother-in-law knew someone at Goodison at the time, and he let slip that after what happened I might well be prepared to come back to England – and join Everton. Billy Bingham was the manager there and he acted on the info very fast. In fact, he signed two of us on the same day: myself and Bruce Rioch from Derby. Billy felt that we'd provide the crucial missing links in his plans to reassert Everton as a major force. Unfortunately, he got fired within a month, before he could actually do anything else!

Bingham's replacement, the oft-reviled Gordon Lee, didn't quite have the same feel for McKenzie's unpredictable charisma.

> Er, he wasn't a fan of mine at all, to say the least! But it didn't spoil my enjoyment of the place and fans. They were wonderful times really. We would play in front of huge crowds virtually every week and playing on Merseyside was totally different to being anywhere else. And the camaraderie between all the players was something very special. We had some right characters at Goodison. Terry Darracott was really lively and chatty, always up to something in the dressing-room. Andy King was also brilliant to have around the place, a great laugh. He'd make himself a mixture of gin, vodka, tomato sauce and God knows what else in a pint glass, and then down the lot in just five seconds! It would make me ill just watching him!
>
> And then there was Mike Pejic, who was, shall we say, very 'different'. He bought Kevin Keegan's house halfway up a mountain in

Wales and seemed to love the country more than the city. And he was a right eccentric. I remember when both of us went away on tour with the England party once, when the late Joe Mercer was in charge. Mike went and disappeared for 24 hours. Nobody knew where he'd gotten to and we couldn't find him anywhere. Eventually he came back to the hotel and when Joe asked him where he'd been, Mike just said he'd been out bird-spotting! He'd found himself a suitable spot, built a little wooden hut and was just sitting there with his binoculars!

And there was 'Fat Latch' [Bob Latchford]. He was truly amazing. Personally, I can never really remember any particular goals I scored, but Bob . . . I think he recalls every one he scored, and there were quite a few of them, especially at Everton. I really admire his single-mindedness. He was totally dedicated to one thing – scoring goals. He took it as a personal affront if a goalie made a save. There were times when he was so incensed at a goalkeeper that I thought he would punch him out! Bob believed he had only one purpose on a football pitch and that was to score goals. If we lost 5–1, as long as Bob got our one then he was happy enough. I know it sounds strange, but that's the way he was. Goals were his business, and even if we lost heavily as long as he'd done his job and scored then that was all that mattered to him.

The other great thing is that you always knew when it was half-time, even if you didn't hear the ref's whistle, because that was the only time Bob would move!

Despite being involved in an unsuccessful period for the Blues, McKenzie looks back with great affection on his time at the club.

The team spirit was always excellent, there was a wonderful camaraderie between the players and we were playing in front of huge crowds every week. In fact it was a great time to be playing football. I really think it was the very best era to be a footballer. We were in-between the naïveté of the '60s and the incredible high-profile pressure that began in the '80s. We were the last era of players I think to genuinely enjoy our footie. We were stress free and it showed. Still, there was a certain cynicism in the game even back then, and certain players got away almost literally with murder on the pitch, because media coverage was considerably less in those days, and it was easier to break the rules without being caught.

I also think it helped that we played on some wonderful pitches, which encouraged good football. Mind you, there were also some right bloody shit-holes. And when I was at Leeds I do remember Jimmy Armfield, my manager at the time, saying to me in December, 'Right, that's you finished for the season, son. The pitches are getting very muddy, so we'll have to put you back in cotton wool until the spring!

McKenzie's departure from Everton was as inevitable for him as it was sad for the fans. The player himself feels that he was simply pushed out. He says: 'Gordon Lee bought Mickey Walsh from Blackpool and bluntly said that he was not going to play me whatever happens. Frankly, he forced me out of the club. I was given no option but to leave.'

McKenzie joined Chelsea for £165,000 in 1978, and it was when he came to Goodison with his new club that McKenzie was made to realise how much he was still loved by the fans.

When the Chelsea team coach pulled into Goodison Road, there must have been 3,000 fans all cheering my name. It was quite touching. Brian Mears, the Chelsea chairman at the time, was on the coach and he just couldn't believe it.

I scored that afternoon as well, and I think my goal got the biggest cheer of the match. Mind you, everyone was happy. I scored, and Everton won 3–2!

But McKenzie could never really settle anywhere for long. His colourful career drifted along, taking in spells in the United States and even Hong Kong. When the time came to hang up his golden boots, concluding a footballing life that was strangely unfulfilled despite his popularity and talent, McKenzie had no real plan of what he wanted to do next. Certainly, staying in the game didn't seem an option to him.

My wife had flower shops in Liverpool, so I got involved with that business at first. Then things started to pick up in the mid-'80s. Radio 5 contacted me and asked, right out of the blue, if I'd do summaries at commentary games. Then Sky Sports wanted me to join their team of pundits. And I also became part of the after-dinner circuit, from which I still do very well.

But McKenzie, aside from all this media activity, also made a brief comeback at Goodison, being the frontman for Everton TV, the station that broadcasts around the ground on match days, in the season 1996–97.

I think the club saw me as a tongue-in-cheek mickey-taker, which was fine by me. You see, being an ex-pro I can get away with any awful lot more than journalists can. I can be harder on players, without necessarily upsetting them.

I've never had any formal television training, but I pick up things as I go along. I learn on the job.

After a year, though, the club decided to move on and try a different approach for the TV station, something which McKenzie accepts with an insouciant shrug of the shoulders. He says: 'I got a very nice letter from them thanking me for all my efforts and just saying they wanted to try a different approach. Actually, I didn't mind at all. I'm just so busy with other media commitments.'

But what of today's players? Does McKenzie, from the media viewpoint, have any time for them. In spite of feeling that he played in the best of all eras, McKenzie has a lot of time for today's players.

They have so much attention focused on them that it can really cause them problems, but by and large they're no different to the lads in my day. And I know players can get reputations for being awkward and uncooperative, but I find that if you treat them OK then they'll respond in the right way.

But one thing McKenzie cannot stand about the modern game is the constant whining over the number of matches they have to play. He says: 'I'd have quite happily played every day, I just loved playing, that's why I can't understand why today's players and managers moan so much about the number of matches they're forced to play in any given season.'

McKenzie is one of life's full-blooded characters, a man who gives the impression of being free and easy, but deep down there's a professional pride in everything he's ever done – and that was never more clearly illustrated than during the period when he lit up Goodison Park with his precocious skills and audacious attitude. He says: 'Maybe if I'd been more disciplined then I'd have gotten further in the game. But then I wouldn't have been me, would I?'

Wistfully, one is forced to wonder what might have been for Duncan McKenzie if Bingham had not been sacked so quickly after signing him. We'll never know the answer to that poser of course, but whenever McKenzie's fitful contribution to the history of Everton is called into question, just recall the FA Cup third round. January 1978. Everton versus Stoke City. More to the point, McKenzie versus Stoke!

McKenzie was in full flight, showing off his whole range of tricks, mesmerising fans, opponents and team-mates alike in a wash of skill and a blur of speed. It was an afternoon when it all came together and for a brief time Duncan showed that he had the glamour, skill, pedigree and belief of a truly world-class performer. That Everton won 2–0 seemed almost irrelevant. We had been privileged to watch a player at the very height of his powers and prowess. McKenzie says: 'Yeah, people always talk about that game being really special. I certainly enjoyed myself that afternoon. Was it the best performance of my career? Maybe, I'll leave that for others to judge.'

That's Duncan McKenzie, a man who still makes light of his own gifts. His two years at Goodison may not have reaped much in the way of silverware, but he left an indelible mark as one of the greatest entertainers ever to pull on the blue jersey.

CHAPTER FIFTEEN

Keith Newton

EVERTON PLAYING CAREER: 1969–1972
GAMES PLAYED: 58
GOALS SCORED: 1

Elegant, stylish, unhurried, unflustered, the late Keith Newton was without a doubt one of the great English defenders of the '60s. He was arguably the natural successor to the legendary Ray Wilson at left-back for both Everton and England, and yet his three years at Goodison Park never quite scaled the heights expected.

It was November 1969. After nearly a decade at Blackburn, during which time he'd picked up a number of England caps, Newton was taken by surprise when he suddenly found himself on the way to Goodison Park. Everton were challenging strongly for the championship, matching Leeds stride for stride, when Harry Catterick decided he needed to reinforce his defence, in particular the left-back slot. He turned his sights on Newton. Nobody was more shocked than the player himself.

> To be honest I was very happy at Ewood Park. I'd just signed a new three-year contract and saw no reason to leave the club. Then Johnny Carey, who was at Blackburn as an advisor, told me after training one day that the manager Eddie Quigley wanted to see me. Eddie said that Everton were interested in signing me, and that Blackburn had accepted an offer of £80,000. In short, he told me that Blackburn were ready to let me go.
>
> I was totally stunned. I told Eddie that I didn't want to go. I had no desire to even go and talk to Everton. But eventually, and very reluctantly, I was persuaded to meet up with Harry Catterick. I think Blackburn at the time needed the money, that's why they were so keen on seeing me go.

Newton went to Goodison and met up with Catterick, but he was not impressed with what was on offer initially.

Financially I wouldn't have been any better off with their original offer than I was at Blackburn, and I told Harry that. So, I turned it down flat and went back to Ewood Park, fully expecting that this would be the last I'd hear of the transfer. But Everton came back a week later with a much improved offer, and I signed.

The new full-back arrived at Goodison, and immediately slotted in at left-back, replacing the luckless Sandy Brown and playing 12 successive games, before the first of a series of niggling injuries that were to blight his time at the club, forced him to miss crucial games.

Obviously it wasn't difficult for me to settle in at the club, because I knew so many of the players from various England get-togethers. People like Brian Labone, Alan Ball, Gordon West and Tommy Wright were regulars in the squad at the time, so there wasn't a problem getting settled in with Everton.

I normally roomed with Johnny Morrissey, who was fine apart from the fact that he used to snore a lot. It was really irritating, because it meant that the next day I'd be knackered from lack of sleep, which wasn't exactly good preparation for a big match. Poor old Johnny did his best to cure the problem, he even tried taking tablets, but whatever he did he couldn't cure his snoring! I just had to live with it.

I got along particularly well with Howard Kendall and Alan Ball. The three of us would go out for breakfast in Knotty Ash after training every morning at Bellefield, and we really hit it off.

In his first season with the club, Newton played a major part in helping the club to secure their first championship since 1963. It was truly a team of great talents, but it wasn't to last very long.

People always wonder why the team broke up so early. After all, you look at the ages of the players, and most of them were in their mid-20s with the best years of their career ahead. That should have been the start of a great era for Everton, yet it never happened. Perhaps it was because Harry Catterick wasn't very good at building on success. He could get one-off teams together to win championships or cups, as his track record proved, but he just didn't seem to have what it took to capitalise on these successes the way that Don Revie, Bill Shankly and Matt Busby could. Maybe that stopped him ultimately being a great manager.

We should really have reached at least the semi-finals of the European Cup in 1971, and who knows, maybe we'd have gone on to the final itself. But we drew the Greek side Panathinaikos in the quarter-finals. The first leg was at Goodison, and although we didn't play very well, we should have buried them. We had so many chances, but just could not score. In the end we had to settle for a 1–1 draw, thanks to a very late goal from David Johnson, and we could only get a 0–0 draw out in Greece, which put us out of the cup on the away-goals rule.

That same year, we also had the bitter disappointment of losing to the old enemy Liverpool in the FA Cup semi-final. Bally gave us the lead and we led 1–0 at half-time, but then Liverpool scored twice in the second half. It was a bitter pill to swallow for the players as well as the fans.

By November 1971, Alan Ball had departed in a shock transfer to Arsenal, and the 1970 team Catterick had carefully nurtured was starting to break up.

To be honest, Alan was a fabulous player, but by the time he left he'd driven us all mad with his incessant moaning. He was really whingeing at all of us. I remember during one game at Elland Road, we conceded a goal and Bally came racing back to have a right go at the defence. We just felt that was totally uncalled for, and that he'd be better occupied getting back up the pitch and doing his own job. So when he left the club it wasn't a shock to any of us. It was almost a relief. The fans obviously didn't see things that way, but with all due respect to him, Alan Ball wasn't very good for team morale.

Apart from watching what should have been a great side capable of dominating the '70s gradually fall apart, Newton had his own personal problems to deal with, namely a constant stream of injuries.

I did have regular problems with various injuries. But the real trouble was that Harry never believed me. He always felt that I was trying it on a bit. Why, I don't know. But that was Harry for you. I would be literally hobbling around, unable to walk, and he still wouldn't believe me. It was strange.

To be honest, Harry was a good manager in many respects, but not in all. He would literally put the fear of god into certain players, and I think that was counter-productive. It meant these players – and I don't want to name them – never performed at their very best. And he would sometimes have a real go at players in meetings, which didn't help at all.

You rarely saw Harry on the training field either. He was very much an office-bound manager. I remember one amusing incident when he was tipped the wink that one of the directors was on his way down to Bellefield. Harry quickly got into his tracksuit and got on the pitch, making out as if it was the most natural thing in the world for him to be out there with us. But, you could see his tie over the tracksuit top. It was very visible!

Newton feels that Everton concentrated too hard on fitness at training sessions.

The training was really hard at Everton, which I didn't mind. But there was far too much emphasis on fitness. Our trainer Wilf Dixon believed in this to a fanatical extent. And whilst I believe that you obviously have to be fit to play football, Wilf took it too far. In fact, things were so hard that players would start to pick up strains on the training ground which threatened to keep them out of the team, which was ridiculous. But again, nobody at the club would listen to any complaints from the players on this situation. There was one occasion when the players tried to persuade Wilf that he was overdoing it in training, but he just wouldn't listen.

Unhappy with the training methods, and beset by constant injury difficulties, Newton never really played to his full potential at Everton. A massive waste of a player who, at his best, was not far short of being world class. And a player who slotted into the England side for the 1970 World Cup in Mexico.

And in 1972, matters reached a head between Newton and Catterick.

It was just before the transfer deadline day in March '72. Harry rang me up and said, 'What am I going to do with you?' I told him that he should either play me, or let me go elsewhere, because I wasn't in the team at the time. Well, that was probably what Harry was angling for. I'd almost been manoeuvred into asking for a transfer. And I was sold to Burnley.

Newton spent the next six years at Turf Moor, where he was relieved to return to a more low-key club.

Burnley were a lot like Blackburn in those days. They believed in pure football, and we did a lot more work in training on the ball than at

Everton. I had a very happy time there. That's not to knock Everton. There were some great times at that club, and the players were of the very highest calibre. It was, and still is, a huge club. But some of their methods didn't suit me, it was as simple as that.

Newton left Burnley in 1978 and played briefly for Morecambe in the Northern Premier League, before turning his thoughts towards coaching.

I applied for a number of coaching jobs, but always got the same reply: sorry, you haven't got enough experience. I'd have thought nearly 20 years playing top-flight football, earning international caps and being in a championship-winning side would have been experience enough, but it wasn't what they were looking for. In the end I just gave up on getting into that side of football.

My wife had her own business, so I helped her out for a while. I also sold trophies to youth clubs, and even got to present some of them as well, which was nice! I would charge for the trophies, but do the presentations for nothing. Then about 12 years ago, I got into the truck game, selling Vauxhall trucks to small businesses and the like. It's something I really enjoy.

As for football, it took a back seat to golf as far as Newton is concerned.

I love playing golf and do so every Saturday, which means that I can't go that often to watch matches. I wouldn't give up my golf for anything, it's very relaxing and thoroughly enjoyable. I do watch football on TV whenever I can, but I don't get along to many games. And to be honest, I was always very bad at sitting and watching a game.

As far as Everton are concerned, I do get along occasionally, but only very occasionally. I get free tickets from the club whenever I want, but it's very rare for me to have the time to get over to Goodison.

To some people Newton's time at Everton was simply a brief interlude between his lengthy spells at Blackburn and Burnley. But it did allow him to taste European football and to be involved with a championship-winning side for the only time in his lengthy and distinguished career. He says: 'There were problems at Everton, I will admit, but there were also some great times and great matches that I remember with fondness.'

CHAPTER SIXTEEN

Jimmy O'Neill

EVERTON PLAYING CAREER: 1949–1960
GAMES PLAYED: 213
GOALS SCORED: 0

Replacing a legend isn't exactly the easiest task in the world. In fact, sometimes it must seem that walking blindfolded and barefoot through a minefield is preferable to taking over from a true legend. Just ask Jimmy O'Neill.

The affable Irishman with the soft brogue was Everton's goalkeeper during the first half of the '50s, taking over from the immortal Ted Sagar, the man who had been in the goal during the 1933 FA Cup final, Everton's first Wembley triumph, and had been at the club for just a few months short of an astonishing 25 years.

'Ted was a very hard act to follow,' agrees O'Neill. 'He was a superb goalkeeper, and even at the age of 40 kept himself very fit. Neville Southall reminds me of Ted in many ways. And there is very little to choose between the pair on ability.' O'Neill continues:

Ted was a very quiet man off the field. He kept himself very much to himself, but on the pitch . . . well, he just hated conceding goals. He would be very angry with everyone when he let one in. Defenders would certainly catch it from him.

Ted, of course, helped me quite a bit, but then Everton when I joined had an amazing coaching staff anyway. One man in particular, a man named Gordon Watson, he was just incredible with me. If Cliff Britton felt that I needed to work on dealing with crosses, then Gordon would take me out onto the pitch after training and just put in cross after cross to me. His accuracy was just phenomenal. He spent a long time working with me. Whatever the manager believed I needed to improve, he would tackle. Gordon must be in his 80s now, but even up to a few years ago, he would still turn up at Bellefield, Everton's training ground. I owe him an awful lot.

O'Neill signed for Everton after appearing for the Republic of Ireland in a schoolboy international against England in 1948.

In those days, we played England at Griffin Park, Brentford's ground, not at Wembley where so many of the schoolboy internationals now happen. In fact, that game made a bit of history in being the first schoolboy match the Republic had ever played outside of Ireland. I remember we beat England 1–0, which was a great achievement. After all, the whole of our team came from the Dublin area, because that was the only part of the country where schoolboy football was played, whereas England had a much better set-up.

Now, most of the England team that day had already signed apprentice forms with top clubs like Manchester United or Spurs, so very few of them were available to clubs. Which was all to the good for the Irish lads. There were a lot of scouts down at the game, and most of them were looking at the Ireland players. Everton were one of the clubs with a representative at the game. He seemed to like what he saw in me, and in 1949 I was invited to Goodison for a month's trial. But after that ended, the club were not totally convinced by what they saw in me, and asked me to stay on for another month.

When that ended, Cliff Britton told me that the club were prepared to offer me a year's trial, but with no guarantees. If, after 12 months, I hadn't made sufficient progress then I would have to go back home to Ireland. It was a simple as that. But I accepted the terms.

O'Neill faced stiff competition from other goalkeepers at the club.

Everton weren't exactly short of goalies when I joined. Ted Sagar, of course, was still going strong. He was a household name as the first choice. But the club in those days ran so many teams. There was the first team, the reserves, the A team, the B team . . . oh, so many. And each needed a goalkeeper. So, in addition to Ted and myself, there was also Harry Leyland and another young chap called Albert Dunlop, who joined Everton at about the same time as me.

Progress through the ranks was very difficult. You virtually had to rely on someone getting injured before you could hope to move up a team. But in that first year at Everton I got a couple of really good breaks. I actually managed to establish myself in the reserves, which was a terrific achievement. And then, in 1950, I got to make my first-team début.

Not that O'Neill is keen to recall now the first of his 200-plus games for Everton. It was against Middlesbrough at Ayresome Park (long before Boro moved to the Cellnet Riverside Stadium) and . . .

You would have to remind me of what happened. We lost 4–0! That was on a Wednesday. Our next game was at St James' Park, against Newcastle on the Saturday. And because both games were up in the north-east, we stayed there. I played against Newcastle as well, and things went a lot better for us. We came away with a 1–1 draw, which was a pretty good result.

The following season, 1950–51, O'Neill got to make a handful of appearances ('I think I'm right in saying it was ten, all early in the season'), although Sagar was still the first choice. But O'Neill did achieve an unwanted footnote in Everton history that fateful season, being one of the players to appear in the first team during what was to prove to be the club's second, and so far last, relegation campaign.

Yes, that's not something I'm happy to have been involved with. To be honest, the writing was on the wall for most of the season. We really did struggle. I remember that in May 1951 we went to play Sheffield Wednesday at Hillsborough needing to win to stay up. We lost 6–0, although at least I wasn't in goal that day!

On a personal level, the season was also a huge disappointment for O'Neill.

I ended up playing in the B team. My form completely fell away. I was really struggling, and you didn't hold on to your place if you were not playing well, it was as simple as that. The competition was so fierce that you couldn't rely on past performances or reputation to keep you in the team.

Cliff Britton picked players purely on form. He had no favourites. If you were not doing your stuff, that's it, you'd be out. Cliff would judge players on their attitude and performances throughout the week in practice matches. You could make huge progress that way, or drop back.

Competition for places back then was simply overwhelming. Everton had so many teams that there were loads of players trying to impress and get noticed. You had to be on your toes, because there were always other players around who were eager to impress, and hungry to make progress. I'll tell you how much competition there was. In the pre-season, there would be a game at Goodison between the first team and the reserves. The public were let in to watch it, and it was the only pre-season game we ever played at Goodison. And normally, the reserves would win, because they were so anxious to get on and impress Cliff. And he took serious notice of players in these games, he really did.

Relegation did have one positive side-effect for young O'Neill. It allowed him to emerge as Sagar's successor.

We all felt really depressed when relegation became a reality. It doesn't take much to imagine how devastated everyone at the club was at what had happened. We were a massive club, and suddenly had to face up to startling reality that we were no longer good enough for the top flight.

But in the second division, I did manage to get my place back on a regular basis. And I even got to play in an FA Cup semi-final.

That game was against the then all-powerful Bolton Wanderers at Maine Road in 1953. Everton, still in the second division, lost 4–3 to their illustrious opponents.

That game was the most depressing I ever played in. It was a real low point of my career. We actually went 4–0 down at one point, and looked totally out for the count. Then we got a penalty, and Tommy Clinton took it – he missed! Now, being 4–0 down, missing a penalty just seemed irrelevant. But we actually then got back into the game, pulled three goals back in the second half, and suddenly that penalty miss took on huge significance. If Tommy had put that one away we could have forced a replay . . . and then, who knows what might have happened?

To his credit, Tommy has always taken that miss in his stride. People always asked him about it in later years, about how he felt. But he never let it get him down. As far as he was concerned, it was history, there was no use dwelling on these things . . . and that was that. I don't know how I would have felt if I had missed!

But a year later, O'Neill did have something to celebrate, as Everton gained promotion after three seasons in the second division.

It was a fantastic feeling to get promotion. And the game when we clinched it in May 1954 was the highlight of my career. We went to Oldham and won 4–0. We played really well, and I was just so proud to be part of that game.

O'Neill hadn't started the season as first choice. Harry Leyland had played in 14 of the first 16 games, but the Irishman quickly made the spot his own once he got back in, playing in the remaining 26 matches.

We had a terrific team back then. Dave Hickson and John Willie Parker [the latter sadly no longer with us] formed a superb striking partnership. I think they scored something like 50 goals between them in our promotion season [in fact, they scored 56 goals between them. Hickson bagged 25 and Parker 31]. Dave was never afraid to go in where it hurt and had such strength and power. John Willie was the perfect foil, playing off of him brilliantly. Then we had Wally Fielding and Eddie Wainwright, who I thought were top-class wingers, supplying the bullets.

All four of them should have been internationals, but the competition was so strong for England places back then. Dave and John Willie were up against Raich Carter, Stan Mortenson, Jackie Milburn. Eddie and Wally had to displace Stan Matthews and Tom Finney. The English game just had so many top-class players. I also don't think it helped any of the four of them that Everton were not in the spotlight at all during the '50s. We just were not competing for the big prizes. And Dave became something of a nomad. He played for Huddersfield, Aston Villa, Liverpool, Tranmere . . . although he's always associated with Everton.

But we had such excellent players back then that it still surprises me we didn't get any success in the '50s. We had some terrific characters. I played with both T.G. and T.E. Jones in defence, two great defenders. And there was a huge Irish contingent there in the '50s. Apart from me, we had Peter Farrell, George Cummins, Don Donovan, Tommy Clinton . . . There were just loads of us there. In fact, Everton seemed to be the natural club for Irish players to migrate towards.

In recent times, the club seemed to have lost the Irish connection. I don't know what went wrong, but promising Irishmen would come over to England and end up at Old Trafford or Anfield, but not at Goodison, which is a shame, because there's a huge amount of potential over there. I'm really glad, though, that now Everton are beginning to reinvest in Ireland. They have a deal with Home Farm, and this young defender Richard Dunne has already made a name for himself in the Everton first team as a result. So, let's hope it will be the start of another fine era of Irish Evertonians.

By 1956, Britton had left the club, to be replaced by Ian Buchan, a move that did not favour O'Neill at all.

There was a world of difference between the two. Cliff was obviously a fine player in his day [he played for Everton during the 1930s]. He was a hard man, very strict but also very fair in all of his dealings. He was straight and honest with all the players. He expected all of us to behave impeccably, as we were representing the good name of the club, but that was never a problem for us. Cliff didn't drink or smoke, and liked us not to indulge either.

He was certainly a good manager, even if we never achieved that much under him. He did an awful lot for me and I will always be grateful to Cliff.

On the other hand, Ian Buchan didn't have any sort of career behind him as a player; he'd been a physical training instructor before becoming a manager. And it showed in his attitude. He was a total fitness fanatic. All our training was geared towards raising our level of fitness. He did not believe in using the ball much during the week. And we certainly didn't get in much practice at improving our actual skills. Personally, I didn't care for it much. Give him weight training and sprinting against the clock and he was in his element, but as a football manager . . . well, he left a lot to be desired.

One thing that Ian did which bugged all of us happened regularly on away trips. About a mile from the ground, he would stop the coach, make us all get out and walk the rest of the way! It was crazy, but he said it would keep up our level of fitness. So, you'd see us all trooping along with the fans towards Elland Road, or wherever we were due to play that day.

Cliff was far more interested in football skills. He certainly emphasised us having a good level of fitness, but he also appreciated that you needed a lot more to win a game of football. Cliff loved five-a-side, or six-a-side, or even seven-a-side games, where there was a real chance to hone ball skills. In fact, I used to enjoy playing outfield in these sort of kickabouts. I had started life in Ireland as a left-winger, before becoming a goalie. I had only been between the sticks for a couple of years when Everton signed me! Sadly, we got none of this under Ian.

And under Buchan, O'Neill lost his place to Albert Dunlop, a cheeky, feisty individual who developed into an excellent goalkeeper in his own right. Certainly 40 years later, there's not a trace of malice in his thoughts on Dunlop.

Sure, Albert took over from me under Ian Buchan. But he'd waited patiently for nearly seven years to get his break. Albert had joined the club at virtually the same time as me, but found his opportunities limited by the number of options we had between the sticks. He'd also taken a couple of years out to do his national service, which cut him back a bit. And when he got into the side, Albert just took the chance with both hands and played so well that there was no way back in for me. It was frustrating, because I felt that I could do as good a job as he did, but Albert was the man in possession, and he wasn't about to give it all up. I just had to bide my time and wait for him to slip up and let me back in.

Unfortunately, for the loyal O'Neill that never really happened. But when Johnny Carey arrived at the club in 1958, the Irish star felt that the tide was turning his direction. He was wrong. Oh so wrong.

I was delighted when Johnny arrived. We'd played together in the Irish side. And Johnny had also managed the team. And, as we got on very well as team-mates, I felt that he would at least give me a sporting chance. But Johnny went out of his way to prove that he wasn't being biased towards me. And his way of doing this was to go totally the other way and make life as hard as he could for me. I was stunned.

For me, the last straw came in 1960 when Albert lost form for a spell. I felt that now was the chance for Johnny to put me back in the team. After all, Albert was struggling, and it made sense to change goalies. But when I spoke to the manager about this, he didn't agree at all. Johnny told me that it was up to me to prove that I was better than Albert. I was so taken aback that I made my mind up to move from the club. It was obvious that I had no future. Look, I wasn't after any favours from Johnny – I wouldn't have expected any – but at least he should have played fair with me, and he just didn't.

It was very sad for me to leave this club. In those days, players didn't leave clubs anywhere near as often as they do these days. It wasn't uncommon to start and finish your career at the same club. Loyalty was taken for granted. Maybe that didn't always work out in the players' favour, but we never thought in those terms. I loved Everton, especially the fans. They had been brilliant to me, and turned up in their thousands all through the lean times in the '50s. There was, and is, no more knowledgeable crowd in the country that the one at Goodison. They know when a player isn't giving his all, when a player isn't trying. And they also know, and appreciate, someone giving his all in the cause of Everton. They encouraged the team, stuck with us through some very thin times, and also had a great sense of humour. Evertonians are very special people. So, after a decade at the club to have to leave was a real wrench, but I just felt that I was being pushed out. If I couldn't displace Albert when he was playing badly, then I had no future there.

Of course, just a matter of months later Johnny Carey was fired and Harry Catterick came in. Who knows? Maybe if I'd hung on for a little while longer, perhaps Harry's arrival would have been a turning point for me at Goodison. But that's all conjecture. The reality is that I made the very sad decision to leave.

But O'Neill left with one record in his pocket: he was Everton's most-capped international goalkeeper.

I only got 17 caps for Ireland, but that put me ahead of everyone who'd gone before – even the great Ted Sagar. People used to look at me in amazement when I say that. What about George Wood, Gordon West, Dai Davies? Well, none of them got more caps for their respective countries whilst at Everton than I did. True, Dai did play 50-odd times for Wales, but most of those came when he was at Swansea; Gordon and George only played a handful of games for England and Scotland, respectively.

I made my full Irish début in 1952 against Spain in Madrid. It was a very painful experience – we lost 6–0, but my excuse was the temperature on the pitch was well over 100 degrees Fahrenheit, which I was just not used to! Over the next several years, I didn't play very many matches, but a lot of that was down to Cliff Britton. He didn't like letting me go for what he termed 'irrelevant' matches, friendlies and the like. You see, in those days players didn't fly to Ireland, you had to take the boat, which meant even for midweek matches you would have to leave straight after a Saturday game, and even then it would be touch and go as to whether you'd make the connections. And coming back was also a problem. So, there was always the chance that I could miss a match for Everton to play for Ireland. Cliff was never happy about it, and often would refuse to release me. So, the biggest games I got to play were

World Cup qualifiers, but, of course, we never actually made it to the finals in those days.

However, O'Neill's proud record as the most-capped goalkeeper in the club's history has now been superseded. O'Neill says: 'Yeah, that chap Southall has taken over from me, and good luck to him. He's a great goalkeeper, one of the very best ever. But I am still second behind him, and that's still something to be proud of.'

Back in July 1960, though, O'Neill's term with Everton was about to finish. But where would he end up? Amazingly for someone so committed to the Blues' cause, O'Neill came close to joining none other than . . . Liverpool!

Friends at Anfield told me that the club were very interested in signing me. In fact, they were on the verge of coming in for me when Bill Shankly arrived at Anfield. He put any thoughts of a move for me on hold because he hadn't seen me play, and any chance of moving there fell through.

In the end O'Neill didn't end up crossing Stanley Park, but made tracks down to the Potteries and to Stoke City, then languishing in the second division, as indeed were Liverpool at the time.

As I've said, it was such an upheaval leaving a club like Everton, but Stoke were building something special of their own. I got the chance down there to play with such world-class players as Sir Stanley Matthews, Eddie Clamp, who had made his name with the great Wolves side of the late '50s, and Dennis Violet, who played for Manchester United during the Busby Babes era. It was a privilege to be involved with such talents, even if they were all in the twilight of their respective careers. And in 1962–63 we won promotion to the first division, which meant it was a double celebration for me, as Everton were champions that year as well!

O'Neill's time at Stoke meant that he was able to strike up a close relationship with Matthews, who remains a friend to this day. O'Neill says: 'Stanley Matthews and I have stayed in contact with one another and we talk all the time. We had some very happy years together, first at Stoke and then again at Port Vale a couple of years later.'

O'Neill's almost idyllic sojourn at the Victoria Ground came to a juddering halt in a similar fashion to the Everton situation. He just found himself unable to get a game after the club won that hard-fought promotion.

Tony Waddington was the manager of Stoke at the time, and he went out and signed a couple of young goalkeepers. Now Tony certainly wasn't about to turn around and drop them in favour of me, even though neither of the two new boys were doing well for him. He would have lost face in admitting that two goalkeepers he'd personally brought in were flops, so I found myself even pushed out of the reserves. I just couldn't get a game. So, I felt it was time to move on.

O'Neill packed up his bags again in 1963, and headed for a brief stay in the north-east of England, signing for unfashionable Darlington. But this didn't last long.

Stan Matthews had taken over at Port Vale, and in 1964 asked me if I'd like to go back to the Potteries and join him. I jumped at the chance. The people down there are really nice, and it was an opportunity to work again with football folk I knew from my time at Stoke.

Eventually, in 1966, O'Neill decided to hang up his boots and retire from the game, without a clue as to what he might do next.

I never thought of staying in the game. In those days, there weren't the jobs available. Clubs had a manager and trainer, and that was it. Coaching staffs of the size most big clubs have these days were totally unheard of. So, there was very little chance for an ex-player to break into that side of things. I didn't even try, although I would have loved to stay in the game in some capacity, along with thousands of other players I suppose.

My first thought was to get back to Liverpool, where I had my roots. My wife is from there and that's where I felt most comfortable. I bought a house in Ormskirk, where I still live. It's not too far from Joe Royle, whom I see quite regularly. We get on well, and often chat about things at Everton.

O'Neill tried to start up his own taxi business once he was back on Merseyside. He says: 'Unfortunately, this wasn't a great success. After it folded, I just drifted from job to job, nothing especially amazing or notable. I had nothing planned out, so I had no choice. It was a way of making a living.'

Now retired, O'Neill has suffered in recent years from ill health, undergoing a couple of heart operations and a knee replacement. He also got a bad case of thrombosis in his left leg – 'As a result of driving.'

But uncomplaining, O'Neill still looks on the sunny side of life, and has an abiding passion for Everton that the passing years have done nothing to dim.

I go to every home match. The club have been brilliant to me over the years. I always get two complimentary tickets, and I don't even have to ask. They are always waiting for me. Everton really do look after ex-players like me. They are wonderful. I know this isn't the case at certain other very big clubs, but that's part of what makes Everton so special. They really do respect old players.

I get to see people like Derek Temple at games, and of course Brian Labone and Dave Hickson are always there, as they work for the club. And everyone there is just so nice to me and my wife. It still gives me a kick to be recognised by fans when I turn up for matches, and that happens a lot more often than I would expect!

I also got to meet Everton director Bill Kenwright a couple of times, and he took time out to chat to me and my wife. Bill always has a smile on his face and just lights up Goodison. He's a true fan of the club and has time for everyone, which reflects the attitude of so many inside Goodison Park.

So, how does O'Neill react to the ever-changing laws of the game, which seem to make life harder and harder for goalkeepers?

I think it's all for the good of the game, actually. Who wants to see a goalie hold on to a ball for an age before getting rid of it? Anything that cuts down time-wasting in football is fine by me. When I was playing, a goalkeeper wouldn't dare hang on to the ball for long, because otherwise you'd have someone like Nat Lofthouse charging into you – and you didn't want that to happen!

Jimmy O'Neill played for Everton during a difficult period for the club, arguably the most disappointing in the club's long history. But his fortitude, dedication, loyalty and no mean talent helped him to become one of the most-loved figures of the post-war years at Goodison.

He may not have achieved the success of Ted Sagar, Gordon West or Neville Southall, but it's unlikely that any of them actually revelled in playing for Everton with as much gusto.

CHAPTER SEVENTEEN

Mike Pejic

EVERTON PLAYING CAREER: 1977–1979
GAMES PLAYED: 93
GOALS SCORED: 2

He looked as if he'd spent time in the boxing ring with Smokin' Joe Frazier or some similar hard puncher, but Mike Pejic was far from a brain-dead pugilist. Pejic was, in point of fact, a combative left-back who also possessed no little skill on the ball.

Perhaps history hasn't treated the aggressive defender with the respect he deserves, but then that's because much of what he did on the pitch was quiet, unassuming and done for the good of the team rather than for his own self-aggrandisement.

But in the mid-to-late-'70s Pejic formed a unique partnership with winger Dave Thomas (fleet of foot, deadly with the crosses) and Martin Dobson (silky midfield visionary allied to a core of steel) that might have taken Everton by the scruff of the neck and propelled the club to greater glory, had it not been for other factors.

Nevertheless, the left side of the Everton team in those far-off days was a joy to behold. The Bermuda Triangle they called those three – and with good reason.

Martin, Dave and I had a great understanding and appreciation of one another. We hit it off on the pitch and off of it. We shared the same interests, the same sense of humour. We just hit it off straight away. We were the quiet ones in the team. There was another group of players whom we called 'The Headbangers Ball', for obvious reasons. It consisted of people like Andy King, who was a right character. They got up to all sorts of crazy nonsense, but we still all got along fine. There was never any trouble between all of us, and the team spirit was excellent.

I suppose I had a reputation for being on the quiet side, but I certainly got on with everyone. Who sticks out in the mind, player-wise? Well, there was Andy King of course, and you have to mention good old Duncan McKenzie. He was a real livewire. Such a nice guy off the pitch, but a really frustrating and annoying one on it. He was, er, just different to everybody else. But we could have strangled him on so many occasions. He just loved getting the ball and keeping it, playing to the gallery rather than for the team. His talent was unbelievable at times, but he could leave you swearing in despair at him as well!

Pejic joined Everton from Stoke in 1977, becoming Gordon Lee's first signing after he took over the Goodison reins. The defender spent so many years at the Potteries club that he'd become virtually part of the fixtures and fittings at the club.

I'd been at the Victoria Ground for such a long time that it was a real wrench to leave, but I felt that I needed to make the move for the sake of my career. Stoke's policy at the time was to sell off the better players, which was madness if you're trying to build a good team. We'd only just missed out on a European slot the season before – ironically, Everton grabbed that instead of us – and yet rather than trying to buy in better players to improve on our position, the club were intent on doing exactly the opposite.

Given what was happening at Stoke, I couldn't see the club going anywhere. I already knew Gordon Lee from his time at Port Vale, who are Stoke's local rivals, so when he came in for me I was immediately keen to talk to him.

I could also see what Gordon was trying to do. He had come into the club and inherited a squad that had some very poor players in there, players who quite clearly were not going to take Everton anywhere. So he was slowly selling them off, and trying to bring in better players, which was the opposite of what was happening at Stoke. So, it was a decent time to move into the club.

It did take me a while to actually settle down. When you've gotten as used to one place as I had with Stoke, getting used to a new environment does take time. There was a vast gulf between Everton and Stoke. I was used to a small-time, friendly atmosphere, but Everton was like another universe. The club was massive, and acted like it. Which meant that the players were looked after brilliantly, but that we were all regarded as just numbers. The directors always made sure you got the best of everything, but they never made you feel that you were important for yourself, only for what you could do to raise Everton's stature. That's not a criticism, it's a statement of fact.

On the footballing side, Pejic again echoes the views of so many players from that period in praising what Gordon Lee set out to achieve.

I got on really well with Gordon. He was very basic, down to earth and totally honest. You always knew where you stood with him. There was no messing about. If he had something to say, then he would come right out and say it to your face. He never complicated things, mainly because he wasn't a complicated man by nature. And he also had a tremendous coach in Steve Burtenshaw. Steve was the man on the training ground, the guy who made us tick. Gordon was the man in the office. It was a double act that, in its own way, was as impressive as Brian Clough and Peter Taylor.

People look back at Everton in the '70s and regard the era as something of a flop, but it wasn't. When you look at our record, we had a very good run. Trouble was, we didn't win any trophies, so the books show us as being less than successful. But we had a good bunch of lads, we worked hard and we so nearly made it all work.

Like every Everton player and fan, Pejic remembers the 1977 FA Cup semi-final against Liverpool at Maine Road with a pained expression.

We all know that Bryan Hamilton's goal-that-wasn't should have counted. Liverpool certainly thought it was a legitimate goal. They couldn't believe their luck when the ref, Clive Thomas, disallowed it. We were desperate to get to Wembley for the final itself. It would have been a great occasion for the club to have been involved with, a great day out and probably would have galvanised everyone. But Clive Thomas prevented it. I'll never forgive him for making that decision. All the players were livid, as you can imagine. We just couldn't believe it. And would you credit it, Thomas only had the gall to walk into our dressing-room after the match as if nothing had happened. He got a very frosty reception.

Pejic recalls the replay – Everton lost 3–1 – with equal horror.

Liverpool's first goal was a penalty that never was. I gave it away, but I swear it wasn't a penalty. I'll always believe that. But what could we do? The fates were obviously against us, and we were just destined to lose. But that was the downside of life at Goodison, and despite not winning any trophies, we did have some very memorable games. Maybe none was better than when we beat Chelsea in the last game of the 1977–78 season. It was when Bob Latchford grabbed the goals that took him to 30 league goals for the season, which won him a cheque for £10,000 from the *Daily Express*. The atmosphere was amazing. There were fans on the pitch after the game in tears. There were teenagers and older fans just hugging and kissing each other. You'd have thought we'd just won the title! But that was how desperate everyone connected with the club was to get some semblance of success. We were so starved that when something like this came along, the place went mad.

Pejic's time at Goodison eventually came to an end because of injury.

I picked up what was diagnosed as a pelvic injury, but it was in reality a double hernia. So I got treatment for the wrong problem. I lost my place in the team to John Bailey and couldn't displace him. I did briefly get back in midfield, because a few of the guys were in contract disputes, but that never really worked out for anyone. So I was sold off to Aston Villa.

Sadly, Pejic only played ten games for the Midlands giants, before injury finally forced him to quit the game.

Ironically, I broke down against Liverpool at Villa Park, and I was out of action for an amazing two years, during which time Villa won the league championship and the European Cup, which meant they didn't exactly miss me.

During the time I went to four specialists, who each gave a different diagnosis of the problem. But I wasn't happy with any of the medical advice I was getting. I remember that I had an operation scheduled at one point, and Ron Saunders – who managed Villa at the time – was livid when I pulled out because I simply did not trust the diagnosis. In the end there seemed to be nothing that could be done for me, and I had to retire. Years later, I met a specialist who told me that it would have needed just a simple operation to put matters to rights. If only I'd known at the time, but it's no use crying over spilt milk!

Pejic, though, had no intention of giving up the game totally. He turned to coaching.

> I had always been interested in that side of things. When I was at Everton, I had long talks with Colin Harvey, who was the youth-team coach at the time. I was fascinated by that side of things, and it was Colin's incredible enthusiasm that started rubbing off on me. And that's where I've made my career since leaving the playing side.

A brief stint as manager of Chester ('I was sacked after just seven months') was followed by a job working for the Football Association, looking after the youth side of coaching, something Pejic enjoyed greatly. He says: 'I learnt an awful lot from my time with the FA, and was also able to help a number of young lads on their way through the game. It was very rewarding and also valuable experience for me.'

Pejic has also worked abroad, having spent a year in the Middle East working in Kuwait with their local FA. But now he's firmly back in the Potteries, as first-team coach with Stoke. But does he still harbour thoughts of having another go in management?

> Oh yes, I've not given up that idea completely. In fact, I only recently went for the vacant manager's job at Walsall, but Stoke blocked my appointment. I suppose I should feel flattered that the club feel so strongly about me remaining that they refused to release me. But I would one day like to get another crack at a managerial position. But, of course, in football, you never know what's around the corner, do you? You just have to ride with the wind. As a coach you're never sure of your job, because a new manager might come in with his own ideas and people – and then you're out on your ear. But I love football. It's given me so much. And this is a chance to give something back. That's why, in so many ways, my time working for the FA with the kids was so rewarding. It really was working at the grassroots level, and trying to put back a little into the game.

Honest, earnest and still totally committed to football, Pejic exudes a love for football that many others have lost over the years. And you still get the feeling that you wouldn't like to go for a 50-50 ball with this man!

CHAPTER EIGHTEEN

Kevin Ratcliffe

EVERTON PLAYING CAREER: 1976–1992
GAMES PLAYED: 472
GOALS SCORED: 2

Kevin Ratcliffe is unique in the history of Everton – he is the only captain of the club ever to have the honour of lifting a major European trophy.

In 1985 Ratcliffe, still just 24 years old, mounted the stairs in Rotterdam to receive the European Cup Winners' Cup after one of the most celebrated victories in Everton's illustrious history, 3–1 against Rapid Vienna in the final of the prestigious competition. And, says Ratcliffe, this should have been just the beginning of the Blues' domination of Europe.

> People still believe we would have won the European Cup the following season. Of course, you can't prove anything, but I feel we were good enough to have at least made the semi-finals. As it was, the blanket ban on English teams in Europe meant the team fell apart. It was a major blow that cost the club dearly. Players like Gary Lineker and Trevor Steven left. And we even lost our manager Howard Kendall because there were no challenges left for us to face. We were denied the chance to pit ourselves against the best in Europe.

The Heysel Stadium tragedy during the 1985 European Cup final between Juventus and Liverpool led to UEFA imposing an indefinite ban on English clubs competing in the three major European competitions. And Ratcliffe is not alone in believing that this affected Everton more than most, leading to the break-up of a great side and sending the club into a decline from which it is still suffering.

Ratcliffe was in a unique position to view the astonishing history of the club in the '80s: the meteoric rise and steady erosion. An Everton fan as a boy, he was signed for the club by Billy Bingham as a schoolboy. He says: 'I knew Goodison Park, of course, from my days standing on the terraces as a fan. But what really impressed me were the training facilities at Bellefield. The training ground was huge, much bigger than I expected.'

'Ratters', as he became affectionately known, made his début for the first team in 1980 against Manchester United at Old Trafford.

> Gordon Lee was in charge by then, and I got on very well with him. He was unintentionally funny in some ways and had a great rapport with his coach Steve Burtenshaw. They were a double act, like Morecambe and Wise in some ways. And you couldn't imagine the one without the other. In fact, when Steve left I feel that was the beginning of the end for Gordon. Steve was the man on the training ground, Gordon was the guy in the office. They needed each other.
>
> I always feel it's a shame that Gordon is regarded as a failure at Goodison. If you look back at his era, he came so close to achieving an awful lot. Maybe luck deserted him at crucial times, but he was far from the disaster many Evertonians now believe him to be.

Lee certainly showed in the young Ratcliffe.

> I marked Joe Jordan on my début. That was an experience, playing in front of about 60,000. We drew 0–0, and I'll never forget the atmosphere, especially when Jimmy Greenhoff came on as a substitute for Manchester United. The roar that greeted him was overwhelming.
>
> I remember that I got two free tickets for the game, which I gave to my father and uncle. My brother also came along, and stood in the Stretford End!

Having got through such a high-profile fixture, Ratcliffe's next game was at Elland Road: the 1980 FA Cup semi-final replay against West Ham (the Blues lost 2–1). And he followed this with another glamour game: at White Hart Lane against Tottenham, Hoddle, Ardiles and the rest.

After this in-at-the-deep-end start to his career, Ratcliffe returned to the reserves for the remainder of the season. But when Howard Kendall arrived in 1981 to replace the hapless Lee, things began to happen for the Welshman.

Recalled to the first team in the centre of defence (his first three appearances were all at left-back), he failed to hold down a regular first-team place, as Kendall strove manfully to find the right formula to revive the glory days at Goodison. And a frustrated Ratcliffe very nearly left the club, with Ipswich Town front-runners for his signature. Fortunately, he stayed put . . . and the rest is written indelibly across the history of Everton.

Howard had his own ideas and ways of working. It did take him a while to get his thoughts and systems across to the players and to establish a stable pattern. And I think it's fair to say that he didn't realise just how many exciting young players he had inherited at the club, players such as Graeme Sharp and Steve McMahon.

Kendall, of course, bought in seven players very soon after he arrived, a batch known at the time as 'The Magnificent Seven', of which only goalkeeper Neville Southall lived up to the epithet, the rest being quickly discarded. However, Ratcliffe believes these more experienced pros bought youngsters such as himself valuable time in the early '80s.

We were in a transitional stage. The younger players were not quite ready for regular first-team duty, and having the more experienced professionals on hand meant we could be gradually blooded rather than thrown in at the deep end, so whilst only Neville of the seven went on the make a long-term impact on the club, their presence was crucial at the time.

By the start of the 1983–84 season, Ratcliffe wasn't only a first-team regular, and a full Welsh international, but was captain of the club, taking over from Mark Higgins.

Playing alongside Mark regularly in the middle of the defence probably helped me to understand what it meant to captain the club. But whilst it wasn't something I took for granted, nonetheless I always felt that I could do the job. I'd always thought of myself as a little bit of a leader and hoped that I'd get it, but it wasn't something that dwelt on my mind.

I first got the job in a pre-season friendly against Dundee, and gradually inherited the role. Did I have problems with the older pros? Not at all. There were a number of players my age in the team by this point, and I think they were all rather pleased that one of them had been given the responsibility.

Goodison was crammed with characters at the time, none more so than striking legend Andy Gray, whom Ratcliffe recalls with special fondness.

Andy was a real leader. He'd take charge of a bus queue given half a chance. But players like him actually helped me as captain. They backed me, and made it easy to lead on the pitch, because they would never shirk their responsibility. At the other end, though, you had Neville Southall. These days he's known for speaking his mind and being a very single-minded character, but when he first arrived at the club from Bury in 1981 . . . well, monks were louder than him! He was very shy and probably a little overwhelmed by the place. No disrespect to Bury, but I reckon our training ground was bigger than Gigg Lane! But being alongside outgoing people like Andy Gray and Peter Reid probably brought Neville out of his shell, and now you just can't stop him!

I think that was part of the secret of our success. We had just a tremendous team spirit. We were always going out for a drink and a meal together. We were really a tight-knit unit. Even when we lost, we had a smile on our face. Strangely enough, we were never a clique. Whenever a new player came in, we'd take him out for a Chinese meal as soon as possible and make him very welcome.

Mind you, we were never slow to take the mickey out of a new arrival. I remember when Ian Snodin signed from Leeds in 1987, he came to the ground and thought he was really well dressed, very smart. We slaughtered him and brought him down to earth with a massive bump in just a few minutes! But it was all in good part.

Ratcliffe's first season as captain, 1983–84, was to prove one of the most turbulent in the club's history. Struggling in the relegation zone as 1983 finished, there were calls for Kendall to be sacked, but the chairman, board and players stood by their under-siege manager.

Since those dark days, many myths have grown up as to what turned the team's fortunes around. Some point to a Milk Cup quarter-final game against Oxford United at the Manor Ground, when a misplaced backpass by Oxford defender Kevin Brock allowed Adrian Heath to nip in and grab what proved to be the winner.

Ratcliffe, however, believes another game at Goodison helped turn the tide.

We played Coventry at home in a cup-tie. The attendance was really poor, about eight to nine thousand. And when you've got so few fans there, you can see the ones that are heckling you. It's very depressing. But we got a stroke of luck that day. Graeme Sharp played with an injury, and he scored the winner in our 2–1 victory when the ball hit him on the back of the neck! Lucky or what? I think that's when we began to believe that our poor run had ended.

The next three years were filled with success. Two league championships, an FA Cup triumph, that European Cup Winners' Cup achievement, plus numerous near misses. Everton were back among the élite.

We honestly never thought we'd lose. Every time we went on the pitch, we were convinced that we were gonna win. It was as simple as that. You can call it arrogance if you want. But our confidence was sky high.

Ratcliffe's fondest memory of that golden period is the game in 1985 against the mighty Bayern Munich at Goodison. The Cup Winners' Cup semi-final, second leg. Everton had drawn 0–0 in Munich. Now the tie was up for grabs.

The atmosphere was just electric. There were about 50,000 in the crowd, and about 48,000 of them were screaming for us. We just could not lose that. Even the final – in Rotterdam against the aforementioned Rapid Vienna – couldn't match that game! We won 3–1 after going a goal behind. We were one down at the interval, when Howard Kendall made his famous statement in the dressing-room that all we had to do was get the ball in the box and the Gwladys Street end would literally suck it into the net! We went out in the second half and battered Bayern.

Sharp, Gray and Steven scored that night to complete a remarkable turnaround. In just 16 months Everton had gone from relegation candidates to being on the verge of the unique treble of league championship, FA Cup and Cup Winners' Cup in the same season. Ratcliffe says: 'We came so close to pulling that off as well. The Cup final against Man United was just one game too far for us. But what a season!'

Of course, lifting so many trophies nobody is more qualified that 'Ratters' to talk about what goes through a captain's mind as he prepares to lift a major cup in the air to the cheers of tens of thousands of adoring fans. Do you panic that you might be the one to actually drop the trophy in a welter of embarrassment? He says: 'No! It never crossed my mind. Honestly, there's no particular thing that ever occurred to me, except a sense of real pride.'

Ratcliffe took the Everton glory years in his stride, years that also saw him made captain of Wales ('That took me by surprise. What an honour, though, to captain my country'). Yet by the end of the '80s, Kendall had gone, many of the heroes of Rotterdam, of Wembley and those triumphant days had moved on. And age was beginning to catch up with the elegant defender.

> I probably should have left the club earlier than I did. I wish somebody had given me that sort of advice. But nobody ever did. Apparently a major European club did come in for me at one point, but I guess Everton gave them no encouragement and I never heard any more about it. Again, perhaps it was up to me to push it. But I was happy at the club.

When the time came to leave, Ratcliffe ended up in Wales, playing for Cardiff.

> I did start to think about getting into management, although it never occurred to me to take the FA coaching badge, because it was such a waste of time. Anyway, I applied for the Cambridge United managerial vacancy in 1991 before I joined Cardiff, but I lost out to another Evertonian, David Jones.

Ratcliffe did get valuable coaching experience whilst at Cardiff, which has stood him in good stead now he's manager at third division Chester.

> It's a world away from Everton admittedly, but it's a start. I've got some good players here, some of whom could play at a higher level. But the depressing thing is how slow a lot of my lot are in picking up basic tactical ideas. I can work with them a whole week on one particular throw-in idea, and they'll get it into their heads. Then they'll run out for a match on a Saturday – and promptly forget what we've worked out! That's when you realise why they're playing at this level. Still, it's a way for me to learn my trade.

What price Kevin Ratcliffe one day returning to Goodison – the scene of so many great occasions for him – in a managerial capacity? Don't bet against it.

CHAPTER NINETEEN

Alex Scott

EVERTON PLAYING CAREER: 1963–1967
GAMES PLAYED: 176
GOALS SCORED: 26

Although affectionately known as 'Chico' – his swarthy looks give him a certain Mexican cool – Alex Scott is as Scottish as tartan, and as colourful and diverse as anyone ever to come and play football from north of the border.

A right-winger full of pace, guile and ingenuity, Scott helped light up the '60s at Goodison with his flying runs and fulminating presence. Whilst Everton's other 'Scottish Alex' (a certain Mr Young) was unquestionably the idol of the fans, Scott had his own revered place among the greats of the era. And played his role in the first two successes under manager Harry Catterick: the 1962–63 championship and the '66 FA Cup.

Yet, Scott seemed destined to travel even further south than Merseyside when he finally left his first love Glasgow Rangers, and decided to try his luck in the English league.

I was at Rangers for nearly a decade, having joined them in 1954, and really loved it there. But towards the end of my time at Ibrox, I pulled a muscle in my back during a European Cup match and lost my place in the team to a young winger called Willie Henderson, who went on to become a real success at Rangers.

It was a really strange time for me, because I was still playing international football for Scotland, alongside such great names as Denis Law and the late John White, who were, of course, regulars in the English game. So, here I was, playing for Scotland, yet the second choice right-winger at Rangers. I knew that I was good enough to get into any other club side in Scotland, but why should Willie have been left out? He was playing really well, and there was nothing I could do about it. The situation hurt, but back then players didn't slap in transfer requests just because they weren't regulars in the first team.

Scott's abiding love of Rangers persuaded him to bide his time, and kick his heels waiting for his chance to regain that coveted first spot.

I joined the club when I was very young. The great Scott Symon, who was manager at the club for many years, had signed me up; I was one of his first signings, actually. I made my first-team début for them at the age of just 18 and scored a hat-trick! The expectation level was very high, until that back injury put me out. But things were a little weird for me when I was still thought good enough to play international football. I remember that in 1962 I was a member of the Scottish team that beat England 2–0 at Hampden Park, the first time we'd done that for about 25 years. It was an amazing day, but that was just a week after I'd been dropped by Rangers before a Scottish Cup semi-final match! So, you could say I was in a highly unusual position. I didn't like it much. In fact, I didn't like it at all, but I just got on with my life and accepted it.

The 1962–63 season finally brought everything to a head, with Scott coming to terms with the fact that he had to leave Rangers to further his career.

The manager did try to keep me happy, but I finally realised that, at the age of 26, I needed to leave Rangers. It was a very hard decision to make. We had such a great atmosphere and were such a close-knit family at the club that nobody ever thought of leaving. It was very rare that anyone asked for a transfer, but I wasn't prepared to spend the rest of my career settling for reserve-team football. I knew I was a capable player and had a lot left to offer.

Rangers agreed to Scott's transfer request after the club were knocked out of the European Cup Winners' Cup by Tottenham, who went on to win the competition (the first British club to lift a major European trophy).

Ironically, Tottenham came in for me, as did Everton, and it came down to a straight choice between the two clubs. And it looked for a while as if I would end up at White Hart Lane. In fact, I met up with both clubs on the same day to discuss everything and then had to make a decision. I travelled to London to meet up with Spurs manager Bill Nicholson in the morning, and then went up to Liverpool to meet Harry Catterick in the evening. It was all very hectic, and after that I would have just 12 hours to decide. I was under real pressure in some ways.

After meeting Bill I had all but made up my mind that Spurs were the club for me. But then Everton made me a very lucrative financial offer that I would have been mad to turn down. I had a young family at the time, my wife had only recently given birth to twins, so the money on offer from Goodison was just too good to turn my back on. And so I reversed my original choice, and opted for Everton.

When I told Bill Nicholson about my choice, he behaved like a gentleman over it. In fact, he told me that he completely understood why I was going to accept Everton's offer, because I had a young family. So I ended up going to Goodison – and have never regretted it!

Making the switch from Rangers meant that Scott swapped the venerated, fatherly figure of Symon for the rather sterner character of Harry Catterick. But whereas many others found Catterick a bit of taskmaster, Scott almost revelled in it!

I got on fine with Harry, no problems whatsoever. Sure, he was a disciplinarian and laid down the law. But then as manager that was his job, and players have to accept it. As long as you performed to the best of your ability and gave 100 per cent then you were fine with him. Harry was totally straight with players. You knew where you stood with him, and I don't see where that could cause anyone a problem.

Harry was also a very astute man, and brilliant at man-management. In fact, I'd say he was one of the very best in dealing with players and getting the best out of them. I remember that in the season we won the Cup [1965–66], Harry made the move of dropping a few of us in November. Me, Gordon West and a couple of others were just left, no explanations, we were just dropped. At the time, I thought that I was playing as well as I had ever done in my career at Everton up until then. I was astounded when I was left out. I just felt, 'He can't do that! I'll show him.' I think we were left out for three games in a row, before finally getting back in the team, but I was so fired up by then that I actually played the best football of my life. I was brilliant, even if I say so myself.

Our left-back at the time, of course, was the great Ray Wilson, who in my opinion was one of the finest full-backs of all time. And after we'd played against Chelsea shortly after I'd got my place back in the team, Ray said to me that he thought I was unplayable that day. He said he was relieved that he didn't have to mark me. That was one of the best compliments I ever received. For someone like Ray to notice how well I was playing was just fantastic, and gave me such a lift.

But that was a real compliment to Harry as well. It was a sign of his man-management skills. He knew that dropping us would actually give us a bit of a jolt, because when you are a first-team regular, it's easy to become very blasé about your first-team spot and take it for granted. So when a manager just leaves you out for no particular reason, it can have the effect of making you realise just how valuable your place is. Of course, it can have the opposite effect and annoy you so much that you storm into a manager's office and demand a transfer. That's when you have to be very careful as a manager and know your players inside out, to understand which ones will react in the right way, and which won't. Harry was a master at this, and as a result he got the very best out of all of us.

Perhaps the high point in Scott's career at Everton was in 1966, when he played in that celebrated Wembley triumph, which has been so well documented. But his truly crucial contributions came in earlier rounds, when the dynamic Scott was the difference between the sides in tight games. Firstly, there was the third-round tie at Goodison against Sunderland . . .

I knew a few of the Sunderland chaps from my days at Rangers. There were a number of Sunderland players there at the time whom I'd played with at Ibrox. So it was an old boys' reunion in some respects. Their manager back then, Ian McColl, was also somebody I knew from my days in Scotland. Of course, this meant that Sunderland thought they knew exactly how to deal with me, and how to stop me making an important contribution. But it worked both ways. They might have known my game inside out, but I knew all about them as well.

At the time, I was in great form, playing as well as I'd ever done, so I was very confident about the match. But with 15 minutes to go the score was still 0–0. Then I picked up the ball on the halfway line, and took Sunderland by surprise when I cut inside from the right touchline, before cutting back to the line and crossing for Fred Pickering to side-foot in the first goal. After that Sunderland virtually fell apart and we ran out 3–0 winners in the end.

I think what stunned Ian McColl was the fact that, for the first goal, I actually left the touchline. I had a reputation at Rangers for always hogging the touchline, and Ian never made plans for me to do anything else, which meant that I was able to lose my marker and lay on the first goal. Just shows that sometimes you can think you know a player *too* well!

In the sixth round, Everton travelled to Maine Road to face Manchester City during the early stages of the Joe Mercer/Malcolm Allison partnership . . .

In the first game and the replay at Goodison, we drew 0–0, and I remember that the City full-back, a chap called Stan Horne, kicked lumps out of me. He was obviously under instructions to keep me quiet, so he thought that a few swift kicks would do the job. Anyway, the second replay took place at Wolves ground Molineux. And with 30 minutes to go, still nobody had broken the deadlock. Then Stan Horne went to clear a ball, I came in to tackle him, mistimed it and Stan ended up injured. It was all an accident, I didn't have the malicious intent of 'doing' him. But City's Mike Summerbee came racing up to me and accused me of being a dirty bastard. I couldn't believe it! After the way Horne had kicked me for two and a half games, for Summerbee to claim I was the dirty one was laughable. Anyway, that injury seemed to disrupt City's rhythm and we went on to win the tie.

But when it came to the semi-final (against Man United) and the final itself (against Sheffield Wednesday), Scott is the first to admit that he didn't cover himself in glory.

I don't think I did myself justice. Everyone wants to turn it on in games like these, because they're so high profile. But on neither occasion did I really get myself into gear. But who will ever forget that final? When we went 2–0 down early in the second half, it really looked as if it was all over. But we didn't really have any thoughts about having blown a glorious chance to win the cup, because we got back into the match virtually straight away, with a goal from Mike Trebilcock, and that completely altered the pattern of the game. If we hadn't hit back so fast who knows what would have happened? Personally, I think we'd have lost.

Not only did Scott fail to live up to his reputation at Wembley, he also suffered an injury that was to spell the beginning of the end of his time at Goodison.

Apart from that back injury at Rangers, I'd been virtually injury free throughout my career. And then at Wembley I got severe cramp, which was common on the Wembley turf in those days, but after that my calf would never again stand up to hard training. Pace was always a big part of my game and this injury inevitably affected the way I could move.

And I was never again fit enough for top-flight footie. Honestly, I would have loved to have been able to play on for another three seasons at least, but it just wasn't possible. I was breaking down.

And so, in 1967, Scott headed back north of the border, settling down with Hibernian in Edinburgh. But he left Goodison with some very fond memories.

I made some great friends during my time there. And there was a very large Scottish contingent at the club as well, players like George Thomson, Alex Parker, Alex Young, Jimmy Gabriel . . . and, of course, Sandy Brown!

Sandy was my room-mate and he became my butler in a strange kinda way! We both came from Falkirk, but he always remained something of a country boy at heart. And he was the butt of so many jokes at Goodison. You see, he was so completely naïve. I had to act as his minder on many an occasion, trying to keep the rest of the lads from going too far with him. Gordon West and Alan Ball would go particularly over the top with taking the mickey out of Sandy. But you'll never come across a more devoted Evertonian than Sandy Brown. He always gave 110 per cent for the club.

And Scott's most memorable match for the club?

Well, I know it sounds strange but it was the 1963 FA Charity Shield match at Goodison against Manchester United. We were champions, they were the FA Cup holders. And we thrashed them 4–0. It was an amazing performance. By the end we were in so much control that we were just teasing them by playing keep-ball. I must admit that maybe we went too far and probably ended up humiliating United, and that's something no professional should do to another. Mind you, we got our just desserts, because a few weeks later we went to Old Trafford to play United in a league game, and they slaughtered us 5–1. Not only that, but they did to us exactly what we'd done to them: kept the ball and humiliated us by making us run around like idiots. We learned a hard lesson that day!

Back in Scotland, Scott got to grips with life at Easter Road with Hibs, following his £15,000 transfer in late 1966. And, as if by a strange quirk of fate, his boss at Hibernian was a certain Bob Shankly, whose brother was . . . none other than Liverpool legend Bill.

Bob was also a great character like Bill, although he never got the same level of rewards as his brother did. But there were some good players up there at the time. We had Peter Marinello, who would later join Arsenal and was regarded by some as being the new George Best. And also a good striker called Colin Stein [who very nearly joined Everton at the end of the '60s, but would eventually go to Rangers].

We didn't have much success, but I do recall one game that was typical of how miserable playing in the Scottish league could be at the time. We were playing Raith Rovers on a bitterly cold afternoon. I was on the subs' bench and it was cold. I was huddled up at the back of the dug out, trying to keep warm and avoid the biting wind. Anyway, Colin Stein got sent off, and with ten minutes to go we were 2–0 down, when Bob Shankly turned to me and said, 'Can you go on and do a job for me?' Can you believe that? I just said to him, 'Even fucking Superman couldn't do a job for you!' That's when I also thought, 'Who'd want to be a manager under those conditions?'

After a couple of years with his hometown club, Falkirk, Scott finally retired in 1972, but his thoughts certainly did not turn towards taking on a management or coaching role . . .

No, that never entered my head. I did once go to a coaching class at Bellefield, but it was so boring I never bothered going to any others. It just wasn't for me. In a way I'd have loved to stay in the game in some capacity after hanging up my boots. But when I look at some of the managers around today and the pressure they're under, then I'm glad that I never got into that game. Football managers are very well paid these days, and they know what they're letting themselves in for. But it doesn't alter the fact that the demands are massive. That sort of thing was never for me.

Instead, Scott got into the pub trade, after briefly flirting with a business he started up with his brother Jim. He says: 'I was in the pub business for about 20 years, and really enjoyed it, even though I had to work a lot harder than I did in football.'

Now retired, Scott still sees some of his old Everton mates. And although trips back to Goodison aren't exactly regular, he follows the club's results with keen interest. 'My two teams are Everton and Rangers,' he says. 'Those are the results I look for before any others. Of course I still care what happens to the club.'

CHAPTER TWENTY

Graeme Sharp

EVERTON PLAYING CAREER: 1980–1991
GAMES PLAYED: 432
GOALS SCORED: 150

When one looks at the history of Everton Football Club, in particular the goalscoring legends, Graeme Sharp has to be included. He holds the post-war goalscoring record of 150 goals in 432 matches. However, it might have been for another club rather than Everton. A number of top clubs were after him, including Aston Villa, but he chose Everton after both he and his father saw the size of the club. Gordon Lee signed him from Dumbarton in April 1980.

> I had naturally heard about the Everton lads through magazines like *Shoot* and so on, but here was I among players such as Bob Latchford, Brian Kidd, John Gidman and Asa Hartford, who I'd seen playing for Scotland. In that respect it was daunting but very exciting. They were all strong personalities at the club and they were all very helpful to me. Everybody looked up to Bob. The more I worked at the club the more I heard about the legendary number nine shirt and how it was held in very high regard by not only the club but the fans as well. But all I wanted to do was get as many games under my belt as possible.

Ironically, he made his first-team début coming on as a substitute for Goodison centre-forward hero, Bob Latchford, against Brighton in May 1980. And from the moment he joined Everton, he felt very much a part of a huge family.

It was brilliant. I couldn't believe it. After training we would go upstairs and have a drink and a meal together. The lads were very sociable and very friendly and so were the staff at Goodison. In fact for a club of this size and stature that was one of the noticeable aspects of the club. Everybody was there to help me and I found that very welcoming.

The first three years were difficult for him as he was homesick on many occasions. This hampered his career at Everton, and when Howard Kendall took over as manager, Graeme seemed to be left behind in the pecking order in playing for the first team. In fact, at one point he was sixth choice and was getting frustrated. But Colin Harvey kept motivating him in the reserves, getting him to do extra training. Slowly but surely the work began to pay off. Colin kept pushing his name forward to Howard and by the 1981–82 season he was beginning to establish himself as a real first-team member, even though that came about through injuries to other players. Graeme grabbed his chance and he quickly established himself, scoring 15 goals in 27 league appearances.

Unlike a lot of players in general, Graeme enjoyed training. At first it was extremely difficult to adapt as he had only known about part-time activities at Dumbarton. At Everton he was put through his paces by Colin Harvey and found that he was quickly becoming strong all round. When he became a member of the first team, Howard Kendall concentrated more on ball skills than the hard-running style of the reserves. As Graeme points out, when Howard arrived it was 'like a breath of fresh air'.

Even after becoming a regular first-team player, not everything went well. The 1983–84 season saw Everton in the bottom half of the table. By Christmas they were 16th in the table. Howard Kendall was under great pressure from within the club, and outside as fans vented their anger towards him. The low point as far as most people were concerned was the league match at home to Coventry in December 1983. A rather boring 0–0 draw resulted in the fans calling for Howard Kendall to be sacked, but Graeme saw things slightly differently.

That was a bad time for the club. No doubt about it. We were trying too hard to win at times and it just wasn't working. People were calling for Howard's head and there was a very difficult atmosphere within the club. It was no joke playing in front of eight, maybe nine thousand, people all jeering and cat-calling the players. But then Howard promoted Colin to the first team as trainer and brought in Peter Reid and Andy Gray to the team.

People were saying he was mad to be taking a chance on what were regarded as injury-prone players, but we had now got two great motivators and an excellent coach in Colin and we then started to believe in ourselves. When people look back now Peter and Andy are seen as inspirational buys. I don't subscribe to the view that the Coventry game or, for that matter, the Oxford United game were turning points for the club. It was more of a combination of bringing new players in and Colin being promoted. That's no disrespect to the late Mick Heaton [Everton coach at the time], but something had to be done. The cup runs also took our mind off the league problems a bit and we managed to gain confidence in ourselves, which in turn helped us get our league form right. In fact it got to the point when eventually we would go out onto the pitch believing we could not be beaten. On Saturdays we would come in, get changed, roll our sleeves up, go out and win the game. It was that simple. Fortunately we had a couple of years like that.

By now Everton were on the brink of a remarkable era. They played in the two domestic cup finals, winning the FA Cup and losing the Milk Cup, but only after a replay to their arch enemies, Liverpool. The FA Cup final ranked as one of the most-memorable games for Graeme as not only did Everton win a trophy for the first time in 14 years, but he scored the first goal that sent them on their way to that victory over Watford.

There were four FA Cup finals which I played in, and of course the European Cup Winners' Cup final in Rotterdam in '85. It was the first European trophy the club had won. There were a lot of memorable games in that season. It's just a pity we couldn't do the treble, probably because we were so tired at the end.

On the subject of favourite goals, Graeme remembers like most Everton fans the one he scored at Anfield, but he does have many to choose from:

Everybody keeps asking me about that goal. Yes, it was special for quite a few good reasons. Mainly because it was a special strike and in particular because we hadn't beaten the Reds for a long time in nearly all competitions. That's always going to be remembered by Evertonians. There were others as well. The one early in my career against Tottenham was excellent and one against Sheffield Wednesday in the semi-final in 1986 and again against Sheffield Wednesday in a quarter-final at Goodison when we were 1–0 down for so long. Everybody will always go on about the Anfield goal but the one I scored against Watford will always be that bit extra special because of the occasion and what it meant to everyone. Let's face it, not many people get to score in a cup final. It was always great to score against Liverpool and that win helped us on our way to the Championship that season and it was great watching it on TV all the time, but it's the Watford one for me.

In 1985 Graeme was capped for the first time for Scotland against Iceland. His partner was none other than his Everton team-mate Andy Gray.

That was a strange one. Working at club level was one thing but at international level was another. It was very exciting. We were up at Gleneagles at the time preparing for the England match at Hampden and I was told that I was going to play from the start so I was really looking forward to it. Then all of a sudden, because Coventry were embroiled in the relegation battle, Everton had to play them on the Sunday and all the other clubs complained because they wanted us to put a full-strength side out. So I was called back to play against them on the Sunday and therefore I missed the England game. What made it worse was we got stuffed 4–1, probably because we had already won the Championship, and I remember they were really up for it. After the game both Andy and myself had to travel to London to catch a flight to Iceland for a World Cup qualifier match. So the Coventry chairman gave us both a lift to Heathrow in his Rolls Royce as he was on his way to London and we rejoined the squad. At that time it was special for both of us, Andy in particular, as he had come back to international football after a while out of the scene. But because we had done well together it meant that Jock Stein had to give us a chance together which delighted us.

Graeme was already a Goodison hero and was revered amongst his fellow professionals. He was an established Everton player, but in those days youngsters were not pushing to get into the first team as they are today.

I remember very few of the youngsters, although I do remember Ian Marshall, who's gone on to a good career, and I remember Howard buying Neil Adams, who was impressive but unfortunately it didn't work out for him. Out of the current players I just about remember David Unsworth as a schoolboy player.

On the subject of breaking the post-war record for scoring 150 goals, Graeme didn't realise he'd done it.

At the time a local journalist told me that I'd broken the record, but I didn't think anything of it as I thought I had more to my game than just sticking it in the back of the net. Naturally I was pleased and very proud when I found out. To think I am next only to Dixie Dean in that respect. It's going to be very hard for someone to break the record. I think the nearest anyone has come to it since was Tony Cottee. Remember, I was at Everton for ten or so years and you don't find that happening very much nowadays.

Most Everton players are upset to leave the club, and Graeme was no exception. Obviously players know that when their time is up sentiment should never get in the way of a great career. In Graeme's case he didn't think he was ready to leave and was not happy about the decision.

I was very disappointed in the way it was done. To be fair I never wanted to leave the club. I still felt I had something to offer, but Howard obviously had other plans. He said he wanted to buy Dean Saunders to team up with Tony Cottee, and I remember speaking to him in the office, and I said to him, 'You're entitled to do what you like, but I think you need three strikers to fill two positions,' as I felt I had a good reputation and I was prepared to fight for my place, and I thought I would still be the number one striker. Howard said that Oldham had been in and that I should go and talk to Joe Royle. I told him that I didn't want to talk to Joe because I didn't want to leave Everton, but apparently they had struck a deal and that I was being pushed out of the door. After a lot of thought and soul searching I decided that I wasn't wanted anymore. I would have been happier if it had come out in the right way and everybody had been totally honest about it. It all happened so quickly. One minute I was on holiday in America and I got a phone call from a friend of mine, and he asked me if I fancied Oldham and I said, no, not at all. When I reported back for training I knew what to expect.

So I talked it over with my family and I spoke to Joe about it. He said that I should take a bit of time. After all, he had been through it all himself. I then discussed it again with my wife and the next day I went and saw Howard and told him that I would speak to Joe about signing for Oldham. He then turned round and said that I couldn't, because they had just sold Mike Newell, and that he was now short of tall strikers. But the decision had been made for me. To leave Everton in that way left a bitter taste and it was sad, really. Everton were a big part of my life.

Graeme found Oldham a bit of a culture shock. Any thought that he would be playing on the plastic pitch was banished. As he admits, he would never have signed if they hadn't put a grass pitch down. He found Oldham a homely club and friendly.

They had just come into the Premiership and it was an exciting time for the club. They didn't have the facilities but there was a lovely feeling about the place which Joe had impressed upon me. I began to enjoy it and I finished my first season there as top scorer with 15 goals. I think I proved a few people wrong. I trained and worked hard. The next year I got a bad back injury which virtually finished my career in terms of playing at the top of my game. But my playing career at Oldham is something that I don't regret.

The next move for Graeme was into management. This happened when Joe Royle took over at Everton.

They needed a caretaker manager. I was coming to the end of my playing career. I had the trouble with my back and I was injured at the time and they came to me and asked would I mind just for the one game. I said yes. They must have thought, that having won a few things at Everton and being experienced enough in that area, the lads there would look up to me. So I did that for the one game, and I thought why not apply anyway as I was at the end of my playing days, really. The thought of management had never crossed my mind but it was an ideal opportunity. I certainly enjoyed it for a long time. It was a very difficult time for the club. We had come out of the Premiership and the team was having to be revamped and a lot of cost cutting had to be done. They asked me who I might need to help me and I immediately thought about Colin Harvey. After all I knew about his coaching methods, he made me the player I was and I had great respect for him. I was delighted when he agreed to join me. I learned a lot about management and I'm very grateful for it. I was probably on a hiding to nothing but I felt it was good for me. In the end I just felt that no matter what I tried to do, the club weren't as ambitious as I had hoped and that's when I thought that I didn't need that in my life and I decided to walk away.

At the time of writing this book Graeme is the part-time manager of Bangor City, who play in the Welsh League.

I was asked if I could help them out and of course I said I would, but only on the condition that if a Football League club wanted me I would be allowed to go if I wanted to. Again it's very different as I'm dealing with part-time players, but if I can pass on my experience to any of them and something good comes of it then all well and good.

As he looks back on his career, Graeme is obviously humble in his love for Everton. He was one of the fortunate to have won the highest honours. His days at the club saw him paired with some great Everton players up front. He particularly liked the understanding he had with Andy Gray. As he said:

Adrian [Heath] and I played naturally together, which is always a good sign. I played with Gary Lineker and we scored many goals but won nothing, but I suppose the best time was with Andy Gray. We terrorised a lot of defences. We had some tough battles with defenders in that time, but with Andy, you knew you had a fighter with you. David O'Leary was probably the hardest one to play against. He was always well organised and he read the game well, whereas I remember Kenny Burns at Leeds threatening all sorts even before a ball was kicked. So, on one occasion, I thought I'd take the first opportunity and I ended up knocking him out. Nothing more was said and I think I got a reputation of being able to look after myself.

So, from being a somewhat shy young footballer from Glasgow to becoming one of Everton's true heroes, Graeme Sharp epitomises what all Everton fans love to see in a centre-forward: height, alertness, intelligence and an eye for goal – 150 in 432 games is testament to that.

CHAPTER TWENTY-ONE

Derek Temple

EVERTON PLAYING CAREER: 1956–1967
GAMES PLAYED: 273
GOALS SCORED: 82

There are certain players whose entire career can be encapsulated in one defining moment, a hint of magic, a shuffle of fate – or alternatively a split second of indecision or embarrassment.

Sheffield Wednesday defender Gerry Young must look back on his contribution to the 1966 FA Cup final with a fair degree of horror. Remember *that* slip? After a virtually faultless performance at the heart of the Wednesday defence, Young took his eye off the ball in the centre circle for no more than the time it takes to bat an eyelid, the ball slithered under his foot . . . and Everton left-winger Derek Temple pounced, strode purposefully towards the Wednesday goal and accurately struck the ball past the hapless Ron Springett. Goal: 3–2. The cup was on its way to Goodison.

Years later, Young himself was still wondering what on earth the left-winger was doing hanging around in the centre of the pitch. So, now is as good a time as any for Temple to clear up the confusion.

I was just in the right place at the right time. I saw Colin Harvey pick up the ball just outside our area. So I moved over towards where Gerry was standing, just in case something happened. It was as simple as that. And when he slipped I just got straight on the ball and ran towards the Wednesday goal. In those situations nothing really goes through your mind. I knew that Ron was a top goalie and would try to cover all the angles, so the only thing to do is make up your mind exactly where to put the ball, and to stick to it whatever happens.

Strange but true. That goal is arguably the most famous Everton scored in the '60s. In fact, there are very few other Everton goals that stick in the mind quite like that one. And it's still replayed and replayed on documentaries about the FA Cup. But there was far more to Derek Temple than one goal.

Actually born in Liverpool, the young Temple was a rarity, a boy from Merseyside who supported neither Everton nor Liverpool. But that didn't stop both clubs taking notice of him when he first appeared on the scene as a schoolboy starlet.

I actually had talks with both clubs. What swung it Everton's way in the end was the fact that I was more impressed with their manager, Cliff Britton, than Don Welsh at Liverpool. I must have been quite serious as a youngster, because I found Don Welsh to be too much of a joker for my tastes. So, in the end I signed for Everton.

That was in 1956. And in the spring of the next year, Temple got his first-team chance, when he was chosen to play at centre-forward, of all positions. But then back in his early days Temple was seen primarily as a free-scoring forward rather than the nippy, crafty winger he later became.

Although he signed for the club under Britton, Temple never got to know him particularly well.

I was only a youngster at the time, so I never got to talk much to him. He was manager of the club, but rarely had any contact with the kids. I did hear him deliver a few team talks, and just sat there in awe, because of his reputation, but he was really only a brief part of my career.

It was Britton's successor, Ian Buchan, who gave Temple his début, and the one-time winger has forthright views on Mr Buchan's style of management.

Ian came from Loughborough College, where he was a PE instructor. He had very little direct footballing experience, and it certainly showed through. I think I'm right in saying that he had a brief spell as a player with Queens Park in Scotland – and that was about the sum of his football expertise before he came to Everton. I'm not sure why he was chosen to manage the club. Maybe the board felt that he could improve our overall physical condition and that our talents would take care of the rest. But it didn't work out that way.

Ian introduced weight training to the club, and other regimes which were designed to make us so fit that we'd have no trouble playing anyone off the pitch for 90 minutes. But, of course, some of the older players did struggle a bit to keep up with Buchan's approach. I can think of Wally Fielding, among others, who had trouble dealing with Ian's approach.

Did it actually work? Well, up to a point I suppose you can say that it did. The first season Ian was in charge we were so fit that we were out in front at the top of the league by Christmas, but then we hit a real problem. Ian's tactical awareness was so poor that we couldn't sustain the effort, and we just fell away. We ended up in mid-table, which was just about par for the course for Everton back then.

If Ian had a better grounding in football skills and knowledge, and could have combined this with his expertise as a fitness trainer then we could have beaten anyone. But as it is, we couldn't capitalise. Don't get me wrong, Ian was a very nice chap – and I'm not just saying that because he's sadly no longer with us – but he left a lot to be desired as a manager.

Temple established himself in the first team as an inside-forward alongside the legendary Dave Hickson during the latter months of 1957, scoring on a regular basis (two goals against Manchester United in a 3–3 draw at Goodison in September of that year was especially pleasing), and he loved every minute of it.

Dave was amazing, a great centre-forward of the time. But he was truly mental on the pitch, a crazy man. There were a lot of dirty defenders around back then, and Dave did not enjoy being fouled. If he got a bad kick then Dave would go all glassy-eyed. You never knew what he might be capable of. He was a bit wild, old Dave, but one hell of a player to have on your side. And he had a great scoring record at Everton. It's just a shame that he never got picked for England, but that was because Everton didn't have the success at the time which would have got him noticed. But that doesn't diminish what he achieved for the club.

Temple's promising career was interrupted by national service and two years in East Africa.

I was actually stationed in Kenya, at a place about 7,000 feet above sea level. But I still got to play a lot of football. Unfortunately, my fitness level dropped so alarmingly that when I got back to Everton in January 1960, I was unable to get back into the first team.

Temple returned to find that Buchan had gone, and been replaced by Johnny Carey, whom he found to be 'very sarcastic', although he appreciated the style of football that Carey wanted to play. And Carey's sacking in May 1961 was as much of a shock to Temple as it must have been for the victim himself.

I suppose every Everton fan knows the story, don't they? About how Johnny had gone to London with John Moores for a league meeting, and in a taxi back to the railway station afterwards, Moores fired Johnny. It's become a very infamous incident. Was it a surprise to the players? Definitely. We had no idea that Johnny's job was even under threat, let alone that he was that close to being fired. It shook us all. But then it proved how ruthless John Moores, as Chairman, was prepared to be to lead Everton to success. He was very ambitious, and determined that nothing would get in the way of the club becoming the biggest and best around.

In came Harry Catterick to kickstart the most successful period Everton had enjoyed since the halcyon days of the '30s. And Temple, for one, had no problems with the new man.

Harry was very strict with the players, a real disciplinarian, but I for one had nothing against that sort of attitude. You must have that sort of thing if you're going to get anywhere in football. There has to be a system, and players have to learn to stick with it. And as long as you were doing your job then he was OK with you. A lot of other players didn't like his approach to the game, but that never bothered me at all.

Catterick was also responsible for switching Temple from inside-forward on to the left-wing, something which gave his career a massive boost, although he regards himself as having been a two-footed player.

During my time at the club I played in every position up front, on both sides of the pitch. I pride myself that I could hit a ball with either foot. That's why it surprises me these days when you hear of players who are only able to play with one foot, and the other is for standing on. If you have a weakness in one foot, then you should be prepared to do whatever it takes to improve it. The more options you have at your disposal, then the better player you'll be. It's common sense.

Temple played at a time of the greatest upheaval in the game's history, when pressure applied by Jimmy Hill and the Professional Footballers' Association led to the end of the 'maximum wage' system. But this didn't result in players being heaped with untold riches. Far from it.

There were obviously a few star names who reaped immediate benefits from the maximum wage being abolished, but for most players it was really business as usual. The theory sounded better than the reality. But it certainly didn't bother me at all. You see, I always felt that, even in those days, footballers were better paid than the man in the street, and we were doing a job that any fan would gladly have done for nothing. So there was a certain degree of glamour attached as well, which was a benefit.

I remember when Harry first arrived at the club, it was just about the time that the whole wage controversy was reaching its climax. Everyone knew it was just a matter of time before the whole system collapsed, and there were reports in the press of how it would lead to financial anarchy. Well, after training one day our first-team coach Tommy Eglington told us that the manager wanted to talk to all of us in the dressing-room. So, we all trooped in and sat down. Anyway, Harry came in and just said, 'OK, I want you all to tell me how much you think you should be paid. And after I've listened to what you have to say, then I'll tell you how much you're fucking getting!' As far as Harry was concerned, the lifting of the maximum wage changed virtually nothing. It was business as usual, and I think the same applied to most other clubs. They treated us well anyway, so they were not about to panic because of this change.

In 1962–63, Temple played a role in helping Everton to their first title since the Second World War, but he didn't actually get a medal for it.

I didn't play in enough games, which was a real shame for me. I got injured in November, and had to have a cartilage operation, which kept me out for ages. But at least I got back into the team for the final game of the season, when we beat Fulham 4–0 at Goodison. That was a great occasion, a real celebration.

It was around this time that the loyal Temple actually became the focus of attention for one of the top sides in Italy, with Sampdoria actually making an offer for him.

What happened was that Sampdoria sent over a scout to watch Alex Young and Ian St John in a Merseyside derby. They were keen on both of them. But as luck would have it, I had a really good game that day and caught their eye. Apparently, they were very keen to sign me, but Harry Catterick turned down their offer. I never got to find out exactly how much they offered for me, and Harry certainly didn't discuss the situation with me. That's the way things went those days. So often you didn't get to find out about other clubs' interest in you until much later. Managers took it upon themselves to make decisions like that without feeling they had to consult a player. These days, with agents involved, something like that could never happen.

Would I have gone to Italy? Well, let's just say that I was very happy to stay in England. A lot of top players from over here had tried their luck in Italy, people like Jimmy Greaves and Denis Law, and hadn't made the switch. So, it was probably for the best that I never went out there. Still, I often wonder if anyone else ever came in for me . . .

But in September 1967, Temple did finally leave Everton after a decade, when he signed for Preston for £35,000.

I didn't want to leave, but Catterick decided to sell me. And he was quite clever with the way he manipulated me into feeling that I didn't have a future at the club. He never came right out and told me that he was letting me go. What he did was put me in at centre-forward replacing Alex Young for a game, then dropped me down to the subs' bench and unsettled me. He made me think that I was gradually slipping out of his plans, and he put the idea in my head that maybe it would be for the best if I was to move on. So, when he came and told me that Preston had made an offer for me, I was quite happy to go and talk to them.

Why couldn't he have just told me outright that he was going to sell me? That wasn't his way. Perhaps he felt that I'd been there so long, it would be better for me to gradually come to the conclusion myself that it was better for all concerned if I moved on, rather than face the shock of being told I was surplus. Or maybe he just didn't like difficult one-to-one conversations with players.

At first I did find it difficult to adjust to life in a lower division. Everton were such a huge club, arguably bigger back then than they are now, that it was a step down. And I missed the camaraderie at Goodison. I made some really good friends down the years at Everton and got on really well with people like Alex Scott, Ray Wilson and Sandy Brown.

And there were always loads of practical jokes flying around. Poor old Sandy was the butt of so many of them, especially from Ray and Gordon West. We had a lot of fun, and when you've spent so long in one environment, it is difficult to leave it and get used to new surroundings.

Temple left Everton with his cup winners' medal and one England cap. Despite his undoubted qualities, the left-winger only got into the national side for one game, in 1965 against West Germany, as Alf Ramsey built up towards eventual triumph in the 1966 World Cup.

Yes, I would like to have played for England more times. But there are plenty of players who never even got one cap, so I'm grateful to have got one game. In those days, national managers would pick provisional squads for the World Cup, and in 1966 I made Alf's list of 40 players, but sadly when he cut it down to 22, I was one of the unlucky players to miss out. There were so many top players around at the time that competition was really fierce, so I never really expected to make the final 22 for the '66 World Cup.

Temple spent three seasons at Deepdale, appearing 76 times in the famous white shirt of Preston, and netting 14 goals, before retiring in 1970. So, what to do next? For Temple management was never an option.

I did have my FA coaches' badge and I could have tried to stay in the game, but I never felt that I would make a decent manager. There are certain types of players who retire from the pitch and move almost automatically into managerial positions. It suits them. But I wasn't one of them. It just didn't suit me as a person.

To be honest, I never really knew what I wanted to do. I started up a little business in Preston, running a post office and shop, and I stuck at that for five years. Then VAT came in and I wasn't at all happy with the way things changed. So I got out, sold off the shop, but in the process, because I was desperate to sell it off, I lost a lot of money.

After that, I had a number of jobs that I never really liked. I had to take them in order to make a living. I worked as a rep for Wedgewood Potteries, but it involved too much travelling and took me away from my family for too long, so I gave that up. Then I went into insurance, before having 15 years as a contracts manager for a double glazing firm. Then, not unusually in this day and age, I was made redundant.

Now, I work for a company who manufacture high-pressure water jets and pumps. I know a lot about building and cleaning chemicals, and work for the firm as a technical advisor and rep. I go around demonstrating the products to prospective clients. If I'm honest the biggest mistake I ever made was buying that post office and shop and going into business for myself. I wish I'd never done it, because I lost so much money I still can't think of retiring.

These days Temple still keeps in touch with events at Goodison.

I go to most of the home games and I do occasionally get recognised, which is always quite a boost. But to me, my playing days were just one part of my life that's now over and gone. Ultimately, playing football was just a job. A glamorous job, admittedly, but a job nonetheless. Still, when I go back to Goodison I do wonder what it would be like to run out on to the pitch and play again . . .

CHAPTER TWENTY-TWO

Dave Thomas

EVERTON PLAYING CAREER: 1977–1979
GAMES PLAYED: 84
GOALS SCORED: 6

Everton fans have always loved nippy, zippy wingers, the sort who supply the bullets for our beloved number nines to fire netwards. In the '50s, the likes of Wally Fielding and Eddie Wainwright lined up the crosses for the incomparable Dave Hickson. In the late '60s, Johnny Morrissey and Jimmy Husband eased the path for Joe Royle. More recently, Anders Limpar supplied Duncan Ferguson. But perhaps none is more beloved than Dave Thomas, the pacy right-winger who played such a crucial role in helping Bob Latchford to many of his goals in the late '70s.

Thomas was unpretentious, uncomplicated and selfless. He was content to sit back whilst Latchford earned the adulation and adoration of the Goodison faithful. But he had his own following, winning over the fans very quickly after his arrival in 1977, and becoming a cult hero to many in those days when the giant shadow of Liverpool threatened to strangle the life out of Evertonians.

Born in Nottinghamshire, Thomas had made his name as a quicksilver winger with Burnley, before spending five years in London with Queens Park Rangers, then considered one of the boldest and most-attractive teams in the country, and during his tenure in London, he was capped for England six times. But in 1977, Thomas took the long road back north to join Everton.

The move from QPR came right out of the blue as far as I was concerned. The club had been going through some changes, with the manager Dave Sexton being replaced by Frank Sibley, and the place seemed to be a little unsettled, but I still never thought that I would be leaving Loftus Road.

However, with Sibley anxious to revamp a team that had come so close to snatching the title from Liverpool in 1976, he readily accepted a £200,000 offer from Gordon Lee in August 1977, as the Everton manager, in his first full season, began to plot the way forward from the previous year's near misses (semi-finalists in the FA Cup, runners-up in the League Cup). He saw Thomas as the man to bring out the best in Latchford.

I had just signed a new contract with Rangers when I got a call, right out of the blue, telling me that the club had accepted an offer from Everton, and that I had permission to go and talk to them. It was a major decision to make, but I talked it over with my wife, and we decided it was worth going for. After all, it was a chance to move back north to Lancashire, where I'd spent so many happy years with Burnley.

Thomas immediately noticed the difference between QPR and Everton.

Oh God, things were done on such a big scale at Everton. They were one of the Big Six clubs back then. QPR were always great to their players, but Everton . . . well, they were just on a different level entirely. I was out in a hotel with my family in Liverpool for three months whilst I looked around for a suitable house. And, at no point did the club object or quibble about the bills. Moreover, they had so many contacts in the city that they would arrange for me to go and see houses. It was so impressive, and something I just wasn't used to.

On the footballing side as well, Thomas found Everton very much to his liking.

I got on very well with Gordon Lee, the manager at the time. He was very down to earth and totally straightforward, but he was a little naïve in some respects. I remember we went away on one trip to Majorca for a mid-season break. Anyway, we were in the hotel, and for some reason best known to himself, Gordon used to love seeing what everyone was eating for breakfast. He would go around the tables just looking. On this trip, Gordon went up to one of the party, our physio, and said, 'What are you eating?' He replied, 'Oh, it's a Welsh rarebit.' And Gordon, without thinking, just replied, 'Oh, it looks like cheese on toast to me!' That's what I mean. He was a man of very simple tastes, and that sort of incident wasn't unusual. In so many ways, he wasn't worldly-wise at all. And every day he provided us with a laugh, without meaning to. But you couldn't fault his commitment and determination.

What I loved about Gordon was that he really wanted us to play good, attractive football. He liked us to keep the ball on the floor and pass it. I know a lot of people now knock him because he didn't bring success to Everton, but he did come very close and had the right ideas. Maybe he lost a little heart by the end, but Everton fans should remember him as a good manager who didn't quite have the lucky breaks you need to be successful.

Thomas quickly forged a bond with fellow right-sided players Martin Dobson and Mike Pejic.

We shared a lot of the same interests off the pitch as well. In fact, I roomed with Mike Pejic. But in general I wasn't one for mixing with players. I liked the simple life. I enjoyed gardening and fishing, and still do. I didn't ignore the others, but I just did not go out of my way to socialise with them. It wasn't me. Still, we did have a good team spirit and there were no problems between any of the players. We had a good squad, and I've nothing but great memories of my time at Goodison. The crowds were wonderful, both to me personally and also to the team in general. Even when we weren't winning trophies, we'd still get gates of 40,000 for games. The fans were amazingly loyal to the club and always believed that better times were just around the corner. They deserved more success than we were able to give them. But we did get into Europe through the league twice in a row during my time there [in 1977–78, the club finished third and a year later, they ended up just a place lower]. And then of course, there was Bob Latchford getting 30 league goals in one season in 1977–78.

The last game of that season against Chelsea was one of my fondest memories of my time at Goodison. Bob needed 2 in that match to make the magic figure, and he got them in the last 18 minutes. It was really special. He got £10,000 from the *Daily Express* for doing it, but he shared the spoils with all the players, which was nice of him. I think he ended up with less than £200 for himself, after everyone had been given a cut, including the groundstaff. But that was Bob . . .

In October 1979, Thomas departed for Wolves in a deal worth £420,000, a decision he still regrets bitterly.

I left Everton over pay, it was as simple as that. I'd had two good years with the club and felt that I deserved a pay rise. I went to Gordon and spoke to him about my financial situation, and he put my request to the board. They rejected it, so I felt that I had no option but to put in a transfer request. That's life I suppose, but I did feel disappointed that the club couldn't see their way to rewarding me for what I'd done, but you have to accept these things and just get on with your career.

To be honest, my career nosedived once I left Everton. I had the choice of playing for either Wolves or Manchester United at the time. Both were interested in me, but I opted for Wolves. Can you believe that? But that's what I did. And I had 18 miserable months there. I hated it [Thomas only played ten times for the club].

In an attempt to restart his career, Thomas headed for Canada in 1980, playing briefly for Vancouver Whitecaps, before returning to England and joining Middlesbrough in 1981, where he appeared some 13 times. But again things never quite settled down as he hoped, and the flying winger left the north-east and headed for the south coast and Portsmouth in 1982, playing for the club until he finally hung up his boots in 1985.

Once he'd decided his playing days were well and truly behind him, Thomas moved into the back room at Fratton Park, getting the job as youth/reserve-team coach at the club, under the management of Alan Ball.

I did pretty well in that situation, and then Alan Ball brought in Graham Paddon as reserve-team coach, which left me free to concentrate on the youth side of things, which I was fine about. I got on well with Graham. But the trouble at Portsmouth was that we kept missing out on promotion to the top flight. And then, when I was 38 years old, in 1988, I was called in to see the chairman. All the staff at the time had contracts coming up for renewal, and none of us knew whether we'd be kept on. There was a huge amount of disappointment about the place that we hadn't got promotion. But I did hope to be kept on. However, I was told that I wasn't being retained. I was further told that the youth team was being scrapped. So, what could I say? I had to accept the decision in the best way that I was able. The chief scout was also offloaded.

But two weeks later, Alan Ball appointed a new youth-team coach: Peter Osgood! So, Portsmouth were not going to scrap the youth team after all, and Bally had brought in one of his mates to run it. That whole situation left a bitter taste in my mouth. Why didn't Bally just come straight out and tell me I was being replaced? Why was I told that the youth team was being scrapped, when that clearly wasn't the case? Of course, it is just possible that the club re-thought their whole plan to get rid of a system that could provide them with a regular supply of young talent. And maybe Alan genuinely thought Peter Osgood was a better man to run it than me. But it was just the cloak and dagger stuff that annoyed me.

I don't believe Alan Ball played fair with me. In reality, he was never my type of person anyway. We got on OK most of the time, but after what happened, I lost all my respect for him. And this just really finished me as far as being involved with football was concerned. I just didn't feel that I wanted to be part of a profession that could treat people in this way. Don't get me wrong, I still love the game, and have great memories, but some of the people actually involved would think nothing of sticking a knife in your back, and those are the sort of people who you can't avoid in the game.

Since that watershed day, Thomas has had little to do with the pro game. He did briefly work on a part-time basis at Brentford a couple of years ago . . .

The manager of the club was, and still is, David Webb, whom I knew from my time at QPR. He asked me to come along and do a bit of work with a couple of wingers they had down there. So, I did that and really enjoyed it, but it still didn't tempt me back into football full-time.

These days I teach part-time at a school in Chichester, doing PE. I've had the job now for about seven years and really it's something I do thoroughly enjoy. But I wouldn't want to do that full-time. My wife teaches at the same school full-time, but it's not for me. I enjoy having time to play golf, and to go fly-fishing one day a week. I've also been coaching a local team for about five years. And during the summer months, I do one day a week coaching at a Butlin's holiday camp.

For Thomas, life is idyllic at the moment, and he has little desire to spoil everything by going back into football full-time.

I'm lucky in that I don't need the money, and I would only really think about doing it if I knew that the person I was going to work for was totally trustworthy, and that's very hard to find in the sport. I do occasionally go and watch games, but I don't miss the involvement – at least not at the moment.

Still, I think football is getting back to good ways and habits, in the way the game is being played, which is very heartening. The '60s and '70s were just fantastic, with so many exciting players around and teams playing good football. After that, the '80s were just awful. The tactical approach changed, with teams going for 'route one' football. The long ball became the norm, and it ruined the sport. Thank goodness that all seems to be behind us now.

Of course, money seems to dominate these days. But I don't regret not being around to get the sort of huge salaries so many players can command these days. I know that some people get worried about the spiralling transfer fees and salaries, but I can't see things calming down. You just have to accept this is the way football is going at the moment.

Of course, you do wonder what some of the old players would have been worth now. How can you put a price on George Best at his peak? I can't even imagine what he would fetch in today's transfer market, nor how much he could get in wages! But I'm pleased that I played during the era when I did.

CHAPTER TWENTY-THREE

George Thomson

EVERTON PLAYING CAREER: 1960–1963
GAMES PLAYED: 77
GOALS SCORED: 1

George Thomson has become one of the forgotten men of Everton history. A stylish, laid-back defender who enjoyed nothing more than playing football – even if it meant giving fellow defenders, his manager and 40,000 fans panic attacks as he calmly dribbled the ball in his own area, inviting calamity.

Not that Thomson was exactly a tenderfoot when it came to tackling. It was just that to him, there was only way to play football: with élan, elegance and just a hint of arrogance.

> The Everton side that won the championship in 1962–63 was just superb. So talented, we could do almost anything. I know it does sound big-headed right now to say this, but we actually went on the pitch for every game genuinely believing we were going to win. No messing, we had total confidence in each other and in our own abilities.
>
> We played some wonderful football. The ability running through the side was just amazing. We were playing the cultured, passing football on Merseyside before Liverpool even knew what it meant! I think, the season of our championship, they'd only just got back up to the first division and were still finding their feet. If you wanted to see classy football, you went to Goodison, simple as that. It was true School of Science stuff.
>
> In a way I was spoilt by being part of that team. I just cannot watch Everton these days, because the type of football they play just makes me shudder with horror. It bears no resemblance to the way I was brought up to play the game, which is a real shame.

Edinburgh-born Thomson spent eight highly successful years at Hearts, winning championship medals and representative honours (although he never gained a full Scottish cap), before switching to the Blues in November 1960, in a deal that also took the legendary Alex Young to Goodison. George was rated at £15,000 in the deal.

> Alex and I were very close. We played together in schools and youth teams. We even signed on for Hearts on the same day – and, of course, we left on the same day. Why did we join Everton? Both of us felt that a move south of the border would do us good. Everton came in, they impressed us, and so we headed for Merseyside.

Thomson was signed by the ill-starred Johnny Carey, who was dismissed inside six months. But the full-back looks back with affection on the man who brought him to Goodison.

> Johnny Carey was a great footballing manager. He just loved playing open, attractive football. His team talks would boil down to, 'Just go out there and enjoy yourselves'. That was it. The man was really a joy to play for, and he was getting a good team together when he was fired in that taxi in London. The whole thing did shake the players. We hadn't seen it coming. It wasn't as if there were rumblings in the club, and that Johnny was known to be jeopardy. But then the chairman, the late Sir John Moores, was a very hard man, utterly ruthless and committed to making Everton a power in the country. He'd do whatever was necessary.

Carey was, of course, replaced by Harry Catterick, a man who impressed in a different way.

> The first day Catterick was at the club, all the players were called to a meeting in the dressing-room to see him. Now, you've got to realise that, at this time, the maximum wage was in the process of being abolished. Jimmy Hill had successfully campaigned for its removal, and now there was talk of salary anarchy in clubs. So, the first thing Harry Catterick said to us was: 'Right, I want each of you to tell me what you think you're worth paying – and then I'll tell you what you're fucking getting!' No messing around. Catterick was a tough customer. He was the boss, a tough disciplinarian, but he got the job done.
> As a footballing manager I personally don't think he was brilliant. He rarely came onto the training ground and there were times when I thought he was a little lacking as far as tactics were concerned. But as a

man-manager he was second to none. He was superb. He handled all
types of players very well. To be honest, he inherited a good team from
Johnny Carey. But he knew he'd struck lucky and just built on it,
bringing in the few players necessary to get us the championship.

I believe Catterick's arrival heralded a change in the club's attitude
and approach. We became more professional, more aggressive and
focused. We started, I suppose, to act like a big club. To win
championships and cups you've first got to believe in yourself. That's
what we started to do, and we still played some wonderful football.

Thomson got his championship medal in 1962–63, but he'd been displaced
by the end of that season by Irishman Mick Meagan, and he was soon sent
packing down to London and third division Brentford.

I left because of injury problems, I suppose. The last five years at Hearts
I'd been an ever-present, never suffering an injury, which was probably
too good to last. But then I came to Everton and injuries caught up with
me. I was off for three months in our championship season with a bad
injury, came back . . . and promptly damaged two ligaments in my ankle.
It was awful. I had to walk in a specially constructed, built-up shoe for
ages. And when that cleared up, I found that Mick Meagan had got a
regular place in the team. So leaving the club was inevitable.

Thomson admits that he could have gone back up to Scotland, but the
bright lights of the big city proved an irresistible attraction to him.

Yes, it would seem strange to leave a top club like Everton and end up in
the third division, and obviously there was a huge difference between the
clubs. But Brentford in those days could field a team with 11
internationals. We had players like Bert Slater, who'd been so successful
with Wolves, and we did try to play first-division style football whenever
we could. But, of course, it didn't always work.

After five seasons at Griffin Park, Thomson quit not only the club but also
the game. He just got fed up with it.

What happened was we had to play Workington on a Saturday, and as
usual we had to catch the 8 a.m. train up to Carlisle, have a two-hour
stopover for breakfast, then get on a coach over to Workington, play the
game, then dash off to get the 1 a.m. sleeper from Carlisle back to
London, which arrived Sunday morning, when you didn't exactly feel

alive. And on this day as usual, it was wet and miserable up there. And I just thought to myself, 'Why am I doing this? I've had enough.' So I quit.

Sadly, Thomson didn't even consider maintaining links with the game.

No, not at all. It never interested me. I just got involved with various business projects. I've always worked for myself, and have mainly been in the scrap metal business, although now I have retired.

Thomson sees very few of his old chums from his days at Goodison.

I've not been up to the ground for years. I did go through a phase of going to see old mates when they appeared in benefit games, but I haven't even done that for years. You see, I don't really have much interest in modern football. I do occasionally watch a game on TV and follow Everton's results in the paper, but that's about as far as it goes.

To me, footballers these days lack personality and character. They just do what they're told, and get paid a small fortune for doing it. Mind you, I can't blame them. If someone had paid me as well, then I'd have been quite happy to do anything I was told by the club!

Back in my Everton days, we had loads of real characters. Everywhere you looked, there were some right personalities. There was obviously a big Scottish contingent at the club, players like Alex Parker and Bobby Collins, which made it easy for me to settle straight in and feel at home. That helped enormously, because although I moved south with Alex Young, he went virtually straight into the army, and so he wasn't around very much in the early days.

I got on especially well with Billy Bingham. We roomed together quite a lot and became great pals. Mind you, I've not seen Billy for ages, at least two years. Funnily enough, although I don't keep in contact with any of the Everton lot, I did bump into Alex Scott only recently. He looked really fit and well, and it was rather nice to talk over old times with him.

Another real character from my latter days at the club was Tony Kay. It's just such a shame what happened to him, with the bribery scandal.

One final mystery, though, needs to be cleared up. It's rumoured that Thomson gloried in the nickname of '007' at Goodison Park. True? He says: 'Er, yes it is. I think I got that name because I came from Edinburgh and had an accent that was very similar to Sean Connery's – and he was playing James Bond at the time . . .'

So, there's no more to it than that?

Well, I did have a roving eye for ladies, I suppose. I've been a bachelor all my life – apart from a 6-week period when I was 45 years of age! – and I do enjoy the lifestyle, shall we say. But that nickname . . . I think I got it from Alex Parker, actually, and I didn't really mind it too much. It's always nice to be remembered for certain things, isn't it?

Perhaps not one of the the names one automatically recalls when talking about Everton in the early '60s, Thomson did lend Goodison a certain glamour that was rarely evident even when the club was sweeping all before it – and for that he deserves a special mention in despatches!

CHAPTER TWENTY-FOUR

Gordon West

EVERTON PLAYING CAREER: 1962–1973
GAMES PLAYED: 399
GOALS SCORED: 0

One of the best goalkeepers to have played for Everton was Gordon West. Like all goalkeepers, Gordon was the sort of character that football needs a lot more of nowadays. He was signed from Blackpool in 1962 by Harry Catterick. It was Harry's first signing and it turned out to be a wonderful one at that.

It was a world record at the time, £27,500. At the time it said in the *Blackpool Gazette* that it would never be broken. I went from £20 to £30 a week and I got a £20 signing-on fee. I thought it was marvellous. Not bad for a lad of nearly 19. Mind you I was a member of the Blackpool first team since I was 17. I actually played in the same team with Stanley Matthews. That was unbelievable. I had taken over from Tony Waiters, who was not in good form at that time, and I played a blinder. Not being big-headed, but I kept playing brilliantly. I remember we had to go to Birmingham. We had to win and Preston had to lose, one of those situations. Anyway I had a great game, Stanley Matthews had a blinder and after the game in the bath, Stanley brought over a bottle of champagne and gave it to me. I'd never had a drink in my life. Mind you I've made up for it since! I'll always remember that moment.

Then I was at Aberdeen with the Under-23s, when I was called back by Ron Suart who was the manager. He said that he would drop me off last as there were one or two others in the car. I couldn't understand it as I was the first one on the direct route. So he dropped me off at my house and he said to me, 'Look Gordon, Harry Catterick wants to see you tonight. He wants you to sign for Everton.' It was that simple. I played four games at the end of that season and I loved every minute.

Gordon quickly established himself as the number-one goalkeeper. The following season Everton won the league championship. Gordon, being just happy to be at the club, got a bonus for being part of that successful side.

I always remember Roy Vernon had gone to see about the bonuses. He came down to all of us and said that we had got it. In those days we were getting four pounds a win and two for a draw. Well when he came to us and said that we got the new bonuses everybody stood up and cheered and clapped, including me and I didn't have a clue what it was about. Now we were going to get a pound per thousand extra people that came to watch us over 30,000. Well, of course we were getting 50,000 at least so it meant an extra £15 on our wages. I'll never forget Brian [Labone] when we had won 4–1. He said, 'What about that goal, Gordon? I saw you counting the crowd!' For me, though, it was great playing with those guys. We had a great team.

When the wage structure was broken in football in general, it didn't make that much of a difference to us. When we won the Championship, in the close season, Harry called me in and said, 'Here you are, a fiver on to your wage.' We never quibbled about it. We were delighted to get the bonus. The next year we would get another five pounds. So within two years, my wage had gone up quite a bit. You didn't argue. You were just pleased that you had done well enough to earn the bonus. It's a different world now.

Gordon had settled in well at Goodison. He established himself as one of the more colourful characters there. Indeed, there were many who were on the receiving end of Gordon's humour, although none more so than Sandy Brown.

We were like one big family and of course there were different characters at the club. Sandy was the one who would get a bit of stick from me. There was the game against Newcastle. I was sent off with only a few minutes to go when the score was 0–0. Sandy went in goal. When I saw him straight after the game I went up to him and said, 'Sandy, when I left the pitch it was still 0–0. What the hell happened?' He said, 'But it was you who gave them the penalty.' I think the only thing he did as a goalie that day was to pick the ball out of the net. So I gave him some earache over it.

Harry was another character. Very strict but fair with it. We were expected to win and if we lost, we would get the verbals off him plus extra training. To tell you of the type of man he was I'll give you this example.

When we used to train, we had a book to sign in with before 10 o'clock. At 10 o'clock the trainer would take the book away. When any of us were late we would get fined. Harry said to me once, 'Gordon, I've gone on about this late business for ages now. Do you know, son, there are people who have been working all night. People starting work at 8 o'clock in the evening and are only just getting home after a hard night's shift.' I never realised that at the time. Through him I learnt that if you can't get to work on time you deserved to be fined. I mean he would let you off once if you were genuine. But it used to happen with the same people all the time.

Another great character was Brian Harris. He was just fun all the time. I always remember the first time I went to work in his car. He picked us up. There was Brian Labone and me in his car. On the way to Goodison, he would stop just before the ground in sight of the floodlight pylons and ask this old fellow, 'Where is Goodison Park?' The old man would go to point the ground out. Three days later he said it was my turn to ask where the ground was. You couldn't refuse to do what he wanted. So I asked some couple, and before the man could answer, Brian Harris leant across Labby and said out of the window, 'It's Gordon West, take no notice of him, he knows where Goodison is.'

The whole team was fabulous. Look at who I was playing with. People like Alex Young, Roy Vernon etc. were all good men. They were older than me and I didn't go out with them all the time. My mate was Labby. We were both quiet in our own way. I mean, yes, we would mess about and have a laugh with some of the others, but we got on so well together. We roomed together on away games in the hotel. We ended up becoming best of friends. I was his best man at his wedding and I also became godfather to his daughter.

In 1966, Everton were involved in one of the greatest cup finals to have taken place at Wembley. Gordon had been out of the side, through breaking his collar bone, since the middle of October 1965. He came back in time for the third round.

I actually should not have been playing in that third-round match. I had broken my collarbone in October and I was still working my way up to full match fitness. I was playing in the 'A' team the week before the third round. That was the week that Harry had taken a lot of stick from fans for playing Joe Royle instead of Alex Young. So, to get the full team out for the third round, I was put straight back into the team against Sunderland. Even though we had won 3–0, I had had a bad game. I got away with it basically. Then, each round from then, I decided I had to do better. So, I played out of my skin for the rest of the season. Then when it came to the final itself, I let in the two worst goals in the world. The first was a deflection off Ray Wilson and I dived the wrong way. All I wanted was for the referee to blow the whistle for half-time. Harry, to be fair, said to keep going and we should pull through. So we went out believing that we could do it and what happens, they go and score again. The ball had bounced off me and into the net. But then we started to play well and really fought back. It was the most marvellous feeling in the world when the final whistle went. What was so fantastic was going back to Liverpool and seeing the people dancing in the street and celebrating.

The next time at Wembley was disappointing, to say the least. Everton lost 1–0 to West Bromwich Albion. But Gordon is quite philosophical about that match.

> We had played them at the Hawthorns ground and beaten them 6–2 and yet on cup final day we just couldn't do anything right. We missed chances, gave the ball away too often and so on. I think that the game could have gone on all night and we still would not have scored against them. It's just one of those things. That's football and you have to live with it.

Gordon was by now at the peak of his career and it wasn't long before Alf Ramsey, the England manager, picked him as the number two to the great Gordon Banks. His first cap was against Bulgaria.

> That was one of my proudest moments ever. I wasn't expected to play that day. We were on the team coach and the boss announced the team. I just sat there expecting Banks's name to be called out as usual when I heard that I was in goal. I couldn't believe it. The game itself just whizzed by. It was a 1–1 draw and I thought I had played not too bad. After the game, I was waiting to get my cap. But what I didn't know was that you don't get the cap until weeks later. So when I was back at Bellefield training ground, I would go and look in the post every day. This went on for about two or three months. Then one day one of the girls said there was some parcel for me, and sure enough it was my cap. I put it on immediately and walked around with it on all day. It was marvellous! I then got another two caps in my career. I played against Wales and Mexico. I've never been on a losing side playing for England. They should have picked me more times.

By the time of the 1970 World Cup competition, Gordon was seen as the number two to Gordon Banks automatically. So it was a major surprise when the squad was announced to go to Mexico that Gordon decided to stay at home. At the time Gordon was quoted as just not wanting to go. The reason was a lot more complicated than that. His marriage was not working out and he wanted to put that before playing for England. Even today, Gordon says it really has nothing to do with anyone. By now Everton were the champions again. They had played some of the greatest football ever, football that any British club would have been proud to play. For Gordon, it was the best side ever.

> It was different from the 1962–63 season. The midfield trio was the best I've ever known. I used to stand back and marvel at the way they played. One of the biggest tragedies was that we didn't carry on winning with that team. We were good for another three years at least, or so I thought. But we never built on the success. Mind you, there were circumstances that may have changed things. Brian Labone was the captain at the time and, with about a dozen games left, Brian got injured when I collided with him in a challenge, and he ended up in hospital. Alan Ball was made captain for the rest of the season and remained so. Alan was such a competitor and I suppose looking back, Alan wanted to win everything and would be very upset if sometimes the players were not turning it on. In the end it became frustrating to all of us that we couldn't carry on winning, especially with Alan as captain, because he was so competitive.

Gordon acknowledges that Everton went on a bit of a slide down the table after they won the Championship. But although the team were not playing particularly well, Gordon reckons he was having one of his best seasons, when he was dropped from the team to make way for David Lawson, an £80,000 buy from Huddersfield Town.

> I remember Harry saying to me that when David was signed that he had to play him because the club had spent so much money on this new goalkeeper. At the time I had never heard of David, so I was not happy about being dropped just like that, especially when I was playing well. The thing was Everton didn't get rid of me for another two or three years. In those days you never got to know which other clubs were interested in you, otherwise I would have wanted to move for the sake of my career. I knew I could still do a great job. Even Everton knew I could, but because they didn't want to be seen to be spending money on a player and not playing him, I lost out. Then Billy Bingham came in as manager and I was told that

I was to start the next season as the number-one goalkeeper, but that never happened because of injury. I was not one for getting injured, but when I was told I was to be put back into the team, I trained really hard and then went and injured myself by overdoing the running. I injured my calf so badly I was out for ages and I never fully recovered enough to challenge for a place. I played four more games for the club and then I retired.

Normally when players retire it usually means they don't play again. This was not the case with Gordon. In 1975, Gordon restarted his playing career with Tranmere Rovers.

That was a weird one, the way it happened. I was working as a rep for Sunblest bread and, to be honest, I hated it. It was nice meeting people but when you are being told to 'go away' nearly every day, it gets to you. One night Labby phoned me and said that he had been talking to Johnny King and that he wanted to see me. So, I went along, not expecting much. I ended up there for six years. I only played about fourteen games, as I was usually helping the kids and playing in the reserves. There was no pressure and I really enjoyed myself there. The thing was I never saw myself as a coach so I never took any badges or certificates, because the way I saw it was that nobody taught me. It was just a case of practice, practice and more practice. If you were good enough you would make it. Maybe a bit naïve in today's game, but that was how it was in my day.

After his spell at Tranmere, Gordon retired from the game he loved so much for good. Of course what better job for a goalkeeper than going into the world of security! Gordon worked as a security guard at an RAF station, RAF Woodvale, near to his home in Southport.

I had a great career in football but really I needed two new kneecaps, so I knew I couldn't carry on. I got this job at Woodvale and I stayed there up until 1996. Then I retired from work altogether as my knees were really playing up. I've had great times wherever I have been and I have played with some of the game's greats, but it all comes to an end sooner or later. I loved my days at Goodison and my relationship with the fans.

The relationship with another set of fans usually made the local headlines more often than the relationship with Everton fans.

Oh God, that lot! Yes, well really when I joined I was just a simple Barnsley lad, although I am very much a Scouser now. I didn't know what to expect. Of course I knew about the rivalry between the two clubs. When I went to Anfield for the first time all I remember was that the Kop were giving me two fingers and shouting all sorts at me. I was really upset because I thought I had done nothing wrong to them. Then somebody in the dressing-room told me to forget about it and that I would get used to it. So, the following year I thought, 'I'll show them cocky sods.' So when I went down to their end, I dropped my shorts a little, blew kisses at them and generally wound them up. Then the following season they were doing the usual two-fingered salute, and then, one bloke came up to me and presented this handbag. I took it off him and began to swing it around. Of course the press got hold of the story and made a big deal about it. To me though it was a bit of fun. I still hate them. No, I'm only joking. It was all part and parcel of being in the game. How I love that club Everton.

Gordon still follows Everton but from his home. He doesn't go out that much as his knees are not in the best of shape. His passion for the club is still very strong. He still sees some of the older players every now and then and he sees Brian Labone more often than that. They are still great friends.

He watches the situation at Everton with a keen eye and insists that Everton have made the right choice in re-appointing Howard Kendall. He also thinks that Everton should move with the times, and he would be delighted to see them build a new stadium to show off to the rest of the country – proof that Everton are still one of the top clubs in the land.

I always thought Howard should be the manager again. He knows his stuff all right. When you look at his career, even at Sheffield United he took them up from probable relegation to the play-offs. He won't do it overnight at Everton but, given time – which the fans are sick of hearing, I know – he will get it right. I still think that Everton as a club are certainly capable of being one of the top clubs. Let's face it, if you were looking for a club that looked like they were on the verge of winning trophies, at the moment you have to say you wouldn't look at Everton. They were one or two points from relegation last season [1996–97]. No one would want to come. I wouldn't blame them, but Howard is a great man-manager and if anyone can persuade them to come it will be him.

Gordon West was one of the greatest characters in the game and Everton were that much richer in spirit with him around. As he says, a simple Barnsley lad who just wanted to play football. He did more than that. He played at the highest level and won medals most would give their eye-teeth for. Yet for him it was all in a day's work. He is truly an Everton hero.

CHAPTER TWENTY-FIVE

Ray Wilson

EVERTON PLAYING CAREER: 1964–1969
GAMES PLAYED: 153
GOALS SCORED: 0

Cool, accomplished, stylish yet terrier-like in the tackle and lightning quick in thought and deed, Ray Wilson would have made the perfect modern-day wing-back – except that his career was astonishingly finished long before that term found its way into football terminology.

Wilson was almost the founding father of the '90s wing-back, bringing an attacking dimension to his play that took opposing teams totally by surprise. Before Wilson, the idea of an overlapping full-back was an alien concept. After he showed how the weapon could be used to devastating effect when carried out by a player with unerring accuracy in crossing the ball to willing targets, it became de rigueur in the tactical planning of most teams.

Perhaps the reason why the Derbyshire-born Wilson was able to develop this role was because he actually started out life as a striker in the mid-'50s with Huddersfield Town, before being converted firstly into a wing-half and finally into a full-back by Town manager, Andy Beattie. And as he moved progressively backwards on the pitch, his career took giant strides forward.

Under Beattie's successor at Huddersfield, a certain Bill Shankly, Wilson not only became a quality full-back but established himself as an England regular, having made his début under Walter Winterbottom in 1960.

But it was with Everton that Wilson enjoyed his greatest years. He joined the club in July 1964 for a fee of £35,000 plus defender Mick Meagan, who had played his part in helping the club to win the championship a year earlier. And for Everton manager Harry Catterick, it was the culmination of a four-year quest to sign up the great defender. He had first made moves to get him when Catterick was manager at Sheffield Wednesday, but the Leeds Road side were indifferent to his approaches, mainly because they had not long since sold off another top line star, Denis Law, to Manchester City.

But, finally Catterick's persistence paid off, and he landed his target, clearly believing that Wilson could play an important role in landing the Blues major honours. And in doing so, Wilson became only the second player ever to play his football under the guidance of both Bill Shankly and Harry Catterick. Only Johnny Morrissey can match that.

However, Wilson suffered a huge blow when, during his first game at Goodison Park against Nottingham Forest, he got a back injury that put him out of action for a cruel four months. He missed a lot of the 1964–65 season, but fortunately made such a complete recovery that he was able to play his part in the red letter year of 1966. Firstly, he helped Everton to FA Cup success against Sheffield Wednesday, and became an immortal two months later when he was an ever-present in the England side during the World Cup campaign that ended with the never-to-be-forgotten triumph against West Germany at Wembley Stadium.

Sadly, Wilson never added to his haul of medals at Goodison. Everton came close, but could never quite scale the heights again whilst the eloquent number three was at the club. Then at the start of the 1968–9 season he got a major knee injury which effectively ended his career at the club. Although he came back into first-team contention, he had lost that edge which made him such a supreme artist at his finest. And in July 1969, at the age of 35 he was sold on to Oldham, one of many Everton players to find a home at Boundary Park during the twilight of their career.

A year later, Wilson became player-manager at Valley Parade, as he joined Bradford City as player-coach. He later became caretaker manager and was then asked to become manager of the club on a full-time basis, but decided that a career in one of the most unpredictable of jobs just wasn't for him. Instead, he wanted something with a guaranteed income – and amazed everyone by becoming an undertaker when he gave up football in 1971! Exactly why he chose this profession remains something of a mystery. Still working at this lugubrious craft in Yorkshire, Wilson is these days reluctant to talk about his footballing career, and defied all efforts on behalf of the authors to talk to him. But his former team-mates remain hugely respectful of the man's prodigious talents.

'Ray Wilson was simply the very best full-back in the game at the height of his career,' says Scottish winger Alex Scott. 'I was always relieved that he was on my side. Facing him could not have been a pleasant experience for any winger. He goes on: 'Ray also had a great sense of humour, although he carried himself almost like a country squire. He was always dressed in a very dapper fashion, with stylish waistcoats and jackets, and acted the part of the English gentleman.'

'I was aware that effectively I was replacing Ray when I arrived at the club,' adds Keith Newton, the man bought from Blackburn to take over his role in the Everton team. In fact, Newton had the double problem of also trying to fill his enormous shoes at international level as well. 'Ray was one of the all-time greats, a player everyone admired. All I could do was play my best, and hope that any comparisons were going to be favourable.'

There's no doubt that Wilson achieved a stature few players are accorded, thanks to his role in helping England lift the Jules Rimet trophy in 1966. But beyond this, his major contribution in helping to revolutionise the way which managers, fans and pundits saw the role of the full-back still has a lasting impact even today, nearly 30 years after he finally hung up his boots and took up a more sedate profession than chasing wingers up and down the line!

CHAPTER TWENTY-SIX

Alex Young

EVERTON PLAYING CAREER: 1960–1968
GAMES PLAYED: 272
GOALS SCORED: 87

There was a certain golden glow to Everton in the 1960s – and much of it was provided by 'The Golden Vision', a slim, stylish Scot called Alex Young.

Perhaps no other player in the entire history of the club has so embodied all the values and aspirations of the School of Science as this remarkably gifted player. As a result, Young enjoyed not only a unique rapport with the fans, but was venerated as an immortal footballer. His name still sends shivers of expectation down the spine, still inspires a sense of yearning. Many players have come and gone and made their mark since Young's departure in 1968, yet despite the great names that roll off the tongue, Everton have never really replaced 'Our Very Own Alex' – and perhaps never will.

Young joined Everton in November 1960 from Hearts, having won championship medals with the Edinburgh club. He came as part of a package deal that also saw full-back George Thomson arrive at the club, but it was Young who was to capture the imagination of a generation of fans. And now he recalls, with a little chuckle, those first awestruck impressions of Goodison Park, after playing his formative years in the more modest surroundings of Edinburgh:

It just seemed so big. It was the first football ground I'd ever seen that had its own lift. And the pitch was absolutely beautiful, perfect for playing on. The whole stadium was just awesome. There was a real atmosphere about the place.

Young was signed by the flamboyant Irishman Johnny Carey, but within just a few months Carey had gone – memorably fired by chairman John Moores in the back of a London taxi – and in came the sterner, more discipline-oriented Harry Catterick. But whilst a decade and a half later, another skilful Everton great would find a change of manager very much to his detriment – Duncan McKenzie was signed by another Irishman, Billy Bingham, only to find his successor, the altogether more austere Gordon Lee, less sympathetic to his individuality – Young seemed to at least find sufficient common ground with Catterick to continue his career at the club.

'The Golden Vision' helped the Blues to the league championship in 1963 and won an FA Cup winner's medal three years later. He is especially fond of the championship-winning side, believing that the team were involved in the best performance given by an Everton side during his lengthy tenure at the club.

> The finest game I played in for Everton came in the 1962–63 season when we beat Spurs 1–0 at Goodison in April '63 and I got the winner [a header that lives on in the memory, as Young climbed gracefully to meet a cross and seemed to hang in the air, before powering home the all-important goal]. Tottenham back then were very hard to beat and had one of the best teams in the country. They'd done the league and cup double only two years earlier, and were a superb team. To beat them proved that we had what it took to win the championship. More than that, though, we *hammered* them. It was a thrashing, but we only managed the one goal.
>
> I suppose that goal would have to rank as my favourite for Everton. You really have to put the whole thing into context, what it meant for our morale to win. That's why it sticks out in my mind so much.

Young's grace under pressure, the time he always seemed to have on the ball, the effortless manner in which he glided and gilded through games making an impact far greater than his energy expenditure would suggest, would have made him a great player in any era. He provided the focus for the hustle and bustle of other less obviously gifted, but crucial players. He was the man who could turn a game with a feint, a shimmy, something different, something extraordinary. Economy of movement allied to a balletic ruthlessness on the ball.

The thrall in which he held Goodison was never more firmly illustrated than in January 1966 when Catterick elected to drop him for a match against Blackpool at Broomfield Road, choosing in his place a gangly 16-

year-old youngster called Joe Royle, who would go on to make a name for himself in later years.

Incensed fans allegedly attacked Catterick in the car park after the match as he tried to board the team coach. Later, the manager himself would dismiss this 'attack' as no more than an accident caused by a crush of people, but he'd been given firm notice that the fans would not tolerate this treatment of an icon, even by someone as respected as 'The Catt'.

The player himself now expresses a mild bemusement and embarrassment at being the unintentional cause of such behaviour, especially as it was never meant to be more than a temporary measure. Young says: 'That was the way Harry Catterick behaved. It didn't matter how much of a reputation you had, if he felt you were being a little complacent then he would have no hesitation in waking you up by dropping you!'

Young, though, was coming towards the end of his tenure at Goodison. And even his appearance in the 1966 FA Cup final was ultimately something of a disappointment, as he honestly recalls.

> I think that was a let-down for Evertonians in general. We didn't play at all well, and just couldn't get our traditional passing game going. We'd certainly played impressively in getting to Wembley – hadn't even conceded a goal on the way – and wanted to turn on a real display, but it wasn't to be. In all honesty, we were lucky to beat Sheffield Wednesday.

Of course, what Young fails to mention is that he was denied what TV evidence has subsequently shown to have been a legitimate appeal for a penalty, when he was hauled to the ground in the first half of a final that still stands out as a classic cliffhanger. But this moment apart, Young didn't do himself justice in arguably the biggest game of his career. And being someone who took great pride in his performances, Young believes that the Cup final wasn't the crowning glory it should have been – despite having a winner's medal.

But this doesn't alter the fact that people old enough to have seen him play believe Young to be one of the true greats of his generation. And the quietly spoken, modest ex-player has difficulty coming to terms with the outpourings of unencumbered adulation he still receives to this day whenever he meets Everton fans, although it is something he does appreciate.

I can't say I was ever really aware of how much the fans loved me when I played for the club. It's not something that ever occurred to me. But I've come to realise what it means in recent years. I'm just grateful that the fans remember me so fondly.

One irrefutable proof of just how revered 'The Golden Vision' was on the blue side of Stanley Park came when Evertonians actually jeered another club player, the great Brian Labone, because he dared to foul the legendary striker. Young explains:

In the 1962–63 season, with the big freeze taking such a grip and disrupting fixtures, clubs were so desperate to play any sort of competitive football that they'd organise matches within the club. We played a couple of games like that at Goodison, the first team against the second team or something like that. Anyway, in one game I was on the opposite side to Brian Labone and he brought me down. Well, the fans did jeer him after that, but I think it was all in fun. Brian was, after all, a genuine Everton hero. Besides, he was what I'd call a kind centre-half. There was nothing malicious about the way he played the game, unlike certain other defenders of the time I could mention.

Young started to fade from the Goodison scene during the 1967–68 season, and by the end of '68 he had left the club, something he now regrets.

I should never have left Everton when I did. There was a certain controversy about the way it happened, but since it involved the manager at the time, Harry Catterick, who is no longer alive, I'd rather not dwell on it.

I went to Glentoran in Northern Ireland as player-manager. But that was at the start of the Troubles over there, so I didn't feel it was safe to stay there. I came back to England and played at Stockport in the third division. But it was a nightmare. The quality of football was so different, so poor after what I was used to that I couldn't adjust. Besides, my knee – which had actually given me trouble since 1965 – was really bothering me, so I gave up playing.

I was 31 years old at the time, which was really too young to retire. And I'd not made any plans for the future, because quite honestly I fully expected to play on until I was about 37. So, I moved back to Scotland, which was a big mistake in itself. I must admit that I've always regretted moving back and I don't think my wife Nancy has ever really forgiven me for doing so!

Not having a trade to fall back on, Young had to make his living as and when he could. But showing the same degree of resilience and insight that so characterised his footballing career, Young went into business for himself.

Of course I had to try and make a living, so I started up my own business. I sell soft furnishings, curtain rails, upholstery and various other accessories to the carpet trade. Do I regret not staying in football? Yes, absolutely. But coming back to Scotland meant leaving the game, and once you do that it's difficult to break back in again. The chance had gone.

These days, Young's interest in football is confined to the lower reaches of the Scottish League – he follows local side Livingston, home and away. But there is a family reason for this commitment.

My son Jason is a striker for Livingston. So my wife and I go to all the games. Jason's 24 and a good player – he was player of the year in the Scottish third division in 1995–96 – but I can't see him ever wearing the number nine shirt for Everton. To be honest I don't think he'll ever reach that standard. But one strange fact that might interest Evertonians is that Jason was in the same under-16 team as a certain Duncan Ferguson!

As for Everton, Young still keeps an eye out for results and occasionally visits Goodison, where he is still certain of the warmest of receptions. There is even a hospitality suite named in his honour.

But for those who stood on the Gwladys Street End in the early '60s, Everton was defined by Alex Young. It was once said that Evertonians wouldn't even have considered a swap for George Best, such was the awe in which he was held. Alex Young has left an indelible mark on the club. His time there coincided with a renaissance in fortunes, as the championship and FA Cup were nabbed, and there were regular performances from him to take the breath away. Even the BBC acknowledged his legacy when they shot a drama-documentary based around him in the mid-'60s called *The Golden Vision*, which underlined the emotional bond between player and fans.

But for all his breathtaking footballing acumen, Young was capped just eight times by Scotland – a miserable international return for such a talent. He says: 'Well, Denis Law was on the scene at the same time, and there were so many gifted Scots around that I can't complain too much.'

Typical, really. Great player, modest man.

CHAPTER TWENTY-SEVEN

PETER REID

EVERTON PLAYING CAREER: 1982–1989
GAMES PLAYED: 228
GOALS SCORED: 13

If you build the ultimate combative midfield player, chances are he'd still come out second best when faced with Peter Reid. A player who never knew the meaning of the term 'to quit', he may not have had the silky touch of others, but what he did have was enthusiasm and a rare ability to get stuck into the fray. If Andy Gray led Everton upfront, then Reid was his equal in the middle of the pitch; no player with even the most modest of intelligence would be prepared to ignore Reid's constant encouragement and determination. He could scare any team-mate into giving that extra ten per cent. And when Everton needed someone to fire them to the heights in the mid-'80s that man was indeed Peter Reid. He should have actually joined Everton from Bolton in 1980 when manager Gordon Lee made a bid of £600,000. But he was sidelined at the wrong time with an injury, and Lee's interest fell away. Who knows what the tenacious Reid might have done for Lee if he'd joined at that juncture. As it was, history reports that Lee made way for Howard Kendall, and the latter wasted little time in going back to Bolton, and securing his man – albeit for a lot less money than his predecessor had envisaged paying!

For a time, it seemed that Reid would be one more of Kendall's transfer follies, of which there were several in the early days. Injuries dictated that the pugnacious Reid expended a lot of time cooling his heels and waiting for his chance. But when it came, Reid was more than ready.

Once he broke into the Everton team in the pivotal 1983–84 season, he gave the first eleven what it had been lacking – midfield backbone! He completed a formidable spine, with Southall in goal, Ratcliffe in central defence and Gray upfront. It was going to take quite a feat of strength to break this spine! Reid's performances were akin to those of Bryan Robson at Old Trafford – a player whom he understudied a number of times at international level. Never beaten, never disheartened, he was the man you'd want alongside you in the trenches. And when the going got rough, Reid always rose to the occasion.

The 1984–85 season was not only Everton's finest, but a personal triumph for Reid, who was named Players' Player Of The Year, a fitting reward for someone whom many undervalued. He rarely captured the imagination, because his style of play was simple, direct and lacking in airs or graces. However, he was far from the unskilled artisan many critics claimed him to be. Reid's vision and authority were almost the equal of his strong will to win. And it was enough to earn him 13 England caps, and a visit to the Mexico World Cup in 1986.

But there are many who believe that he stayed too long at Everton. When Kendall quit in 1987, he became player-coach under new manager Colin Harvey, but his abilities were on the wane, and as Everton went into a steep decline he struggled to make his presence felt. The Peter Reid who drove on the Everton during the glory days found he could no longer make the impact. And the boo boys often got on his back at Goodison – rather unfair when you consider what he'd done for the club. But such is the fickle nature of football.

Eventually, Reid left Everton in 1989 for Queens Park Rangers – a somewhat strange move, and one that did little to further the midfielder's reputation. But his tenure at Loftus Road was brief. He returned to the north-west, becoming player-manager of Manchester City – a baptism of fire for any manager. But Reid handled the task seemingly rather well, taking the club to successive finishes of fifth, fifth and ninth. However, such is the volatile and unpredictable nature of the sport that he was unceremoniously dumped at the start of the 1993–94 season after opening the campaign with a draw and three defeats. Many believed that City chairman Peter Swales made a huge error of judgement, and City scarcely improved in his absence.

After a brief period out of the game, Reid returned in March 1995, taking charge of north-east giants Sunderland. Again he took on a vast task. As at Maine Road he was managing a club who saw themselves a top club, but were living in the shadow of more successful and high profile neighbours. But Reid spent seven reasonably successful years with Sunderland, taking them to promotion and establishing the club as a decent

Premiership bet, mostly spending money wisely on players who could firstly solidify the club's position, and then take them towards a prestigious European spot.

But in 2002–03, everything went wrong for Reid. The club simply couldn't get into gear, and as matches fell away, so Sunderland's points tally began to look increasingly dire. Inevitably, Reid was fired for the second time in his managerial career, and had to look on as, firstly, Howard Wilkinson and finally Mick McCarthy failed to arrest the club's decline. Relegation was inevitable long before the end of the season. Many at the club wonder if getting rid of Reid was the right move at the time.

But the man known in some quarters as 'The Blue Monkey', who had Sunderland fans singing 'Cheer up Peter Reid' at him Monkees-style, wasn't out of work for long. When Terry Venables quit at Elland Road towards the end of the 2002–03 season, the Leeds board turned to Reid. He had a strange arrangement with the club in that he would only get paid of they stayed up, and then would pocket a considerable fortune. He duly achieved the task, and then was offered the chance to take the job on a permanent basis. However, Reid had to watch helplessly as some of his most prized playing assets were sold off, to try and cut the crippling debts faced by Leeds. Once again it would seem Reid is going have to battle with his back firmly against the wall – and at the time of writing things do not look particularly good.

But if there's one thing Reid relishes it is a battle – there is no manager in the Premiership who would be more prepared to take on this mammoth task. That's why he is a valued member of the managerial community, and will always find work. Of course, given his Everton connections, Reid has always been strongly linked with the managerial chair when it has become vacant – and over the past decade or so that been a considerable number of times. Opinion is always divided on whether Reid is the right man for the job. Some believe he has the credentials and also the Everton pedigree to do a great job – others are a lot less convinced. Whatever, he has yet to be offered the job, or even to express an interest in it. And David Moyes seemingly ready to stay for a long while, Reid's chance may well have gone.

It is rather fascinating that Peter Reid is one of only three members of the mid-'80s squad to go into management after their playing days ended. The others were Adrian Heath, who was briefly in charge at Burnley, before heading the call from Howard Kendall to become his assistant when he went back to Goodison for a third term, Kevin Ratcliffe, whose stints at both Chester and Shrewsbury were hardly the stuff of legend. Of the

others, Andy Gray was briefly assistant manager at Aston Villa, and . . .
that's about it. It is quite astonishing that none of the others followed suit.
But then it is a hazardous profession.

So why has Reid succeeded as a manager where not one of his Everton
peers have made even an indentation? Well, as a player he was always
capable of reading the game, and displayed a rare footballing intelligence.
He is also clearly a man able to get the very best out of others. While many
players who've reached the very heights seem incapable of understanding
why there might be some who don't have their focus and abilities, Reid
understands this, and is fully prepared to work with his squad to bring out
the very best they can offer. Perhaps it's the fact that he's always had to
struggle to achieve anything in the game – he was never handed anything
on a silver platter – that makes him so aware of what others have to go
through. But there's no question that he has the mix of calm, cool
perspective and the explosive passion which goes to make the perfect
manager.

It would be interesting to see how he might handle a player like Wayne
Rooney. And he has one or two of that tender age and potential at Leeds.
If he can survive this turbulent period in Leeds' history, then Peter Reid
might finally achieve as a manager what he did as a player. And don't rule
him for the ultimate poison chalice – the England job. He does love a
challenge.

CHAPTER TWENTY-EIGHT

NEVILLE SOUTHALL

EVERTON PLAYING CAREER: 1981–1998
GAMES PLAYED: 750
GOALS SCORED: 0

It may seem strange to some that one of the greatest players ever to grace Everton should be known as 'The Binman', but such is Neville Southall's epithet. Why? Two reasons – firstly he was precisely that prior to making the grade as a goalkeeper (he'd also been a hod carrier on a building site), and secondly he was the epitome of dishevelment, the antithesis of style.

But as a goalkeeper, he was a supreme exponent of the art. At his height, Southall was arguably the best goalie in the world, and certainly the finest not only in Everton's history, but also ever to play for Wales. It remains one of the sad facts of Southall's career that being Welsh he never got the chance to show off his considerable skill, energy and insight on either the European Championship or World Cup stages. Wales never qualified for either, so big Nev was always denied this deserved accolade. However, at club level, the man reigned supreme. He dominated his defence, as well as defying strikers to beat him. He was the master of the one-on-one situation, when you'd back Southall every time against any attacker foolish enough to take him on.

During the mid-'80s when Everton were one of the most dominant clubs in Europe, Southall was crucial, a brilliant last line of defence who performed heroics when necessary, and yet always did this with a certain indifference. Sometimes you wondered if he could actually be bothered.

But the man worked incredibly hard at his game. An assiduous trainer, throughout his lengthy career he never allowed complacency to set in. And when he finally left Goodison Park in 1998, after 17 years at the club, he left behind a void that still hasn't been filled. Come on, how do you replace a legend?

But all of this is a far cry from his rather inauspicious start at the club. Everton signed Southall for £150,000 in July 1981 from Bury (they'd paid just £6,000 when acquiring him in from Cheshire League side Winsford a year previously). At first he was pitted against Jim Arnold in a battle for the goalkeeping jersey, with neither man able to impress enough to make it their own. Southall made his début against Ipswich at Goodison in October 1981, but the young Welshman (he was still only 23) seemed to be finding the jump to playing in the top flight difficult to handle. The last straw for many Evertonians came on an infamous afternoon when arch-rivals Liverpool stuck five past Southall. For many that would have been the end of their career at Everton. And he was swiftly dispatched to Port Vale for what was officially a 'loan spell'. Many believed he'd never return to Goodison, but this period was his making. He played only nine times for Vale, but regained his confidence, and sharpened his skills to such an extent that, upon coming back to Goodison, he settled the dispute with Arnold once and for all – he took the number one jersey and made it his own.

Southall was transformed from being unkempt, both sartorially and in terms of his goalkeeping style, into a formidable character who was at the heart of Everton's rise from the nether regions of the First Division to European ascendancy. His form during the famed 1984–85 season was such that he was voted Footballer of the Year, and there's little doubt that he'd have been England's first choice at this time. As it was, Southall was one of the few shining lights in a Welsh side that never even looked like making its mark on the international stage. At club level, Southall's heroics were simply astonishing. He seemed to be the complete goalkeeper, with scarcely a weakness.

But in 1986, he was hit by a bad injury, one that sidelined him from March. It gave his understudy, Bobby Mimms (one of many to fulfil this unrewarding role during Southall's tenure at Goodison), a chance to shine, but he was not even close to the class of the great man, and how galling must it have been for Southall to watch on helplessly as Everton lost the 1986 all-Merseyside FA Cup final 3–1.

He returned between the sticks in October, in time to help inspire Everton to a second championship in three seasons. And his form seemed to suffer not at all from that injury. What's more, as Everton entered a disastrous period, Southall maintained his form and commitment, remaining among the very best players at the club as the turbulent times threatened to sweep all out to sea.

But, like all goalkeepers, he had his eccentric side. A wilful personality meant that he often acted as an individual. On one infamous occasion, during Colin Harvey's testing time as manager, Southall was so disgusted with a first-half display against Queens Park Rangers at Loftus Road that he refused to go into the dressing-room at half-time, preferring to sit by the goal – much to the amusement and bemusement of everyone.

Whatever his foibles, though, without Southall Everton may well have sunk without trace as the 1990s unfurled. He was by then the last remaining player link to the glory days of the previous decade, but by now he also had various records in his sights. In October 1994 he passed Ted Sagar's record of 432 appearances for Everton in a home game against Coventry City (typically, the Blues lost 2–0). This was during an appalling start to a season, one that threatened to see Everton relegated by Christmas. But, with the arrival of Joe Royle as manager, things turned around in a manner not unlike that of the 1983–84 season. And as was the case with Kendall, Royle managed to lead Everton from the brink of relegation to FA Cup heaven. In the 1995 final Everton faced and beat Manchester United 1–0, revenge for the defeat ten years earlier. And while Paul Rideout was the goalscoring hero, it was Southall's calm, confident, dominant performance in the second half that ensured victory. Approaching his 37th birthday, he showed little sign of slowing down. Typically, he shunned the post-match celebrations to drive home to Wales.

Southall achieved the remarkable record of 700 appearances for Everton at the start of the 1996–97 season against Newcastle, and in September '97 became the first Premiership player to play 200 games. But it was during this period that it became obvious Southall was close to the end of his reign at Goodison. After the dreadful disappointment of the 3–2 defeat at the hands of Bradford City in the FA Cup, Paul Gerrard was given a chance to show he could take over from Southall on a long-term basis. However, all this did was emphasize that Everton could not yet afford to bin 'The Binman'. Southall returned, and played his 750th game for the club at Goodison against Spurs on 29 November 1997 – Tottenham won 2–0. This was to be Southall's last appearance in an Everton shirt. With Norwegian Thomas Myhre now at the club, and given the opportunity to take over as first-choice goalkeeper, Southall was loaned out to Southend for two months, playing nine games (he never finished on the winning side). He followed this with a very brief spell on loan at Stoke, and at this juncture took the decision to leave the club with whom he'll always be most associated.

Southall got the chance to say farewell to the fans before the final game of the 1997–98 season, at Goodison against Coventry. He received a deservedly rapturous ovation on the pitch, prior to one of the most important games in Everton's recent history, when they battled to avoid relegation. How Southall would have loved to have been involved in such a scrap!

Since quitting Goodison, Southall has failed to break into management as he had intended. He played for Bradford City and Torquay, and has coached at Bradford, York, Tranmere and with Wales. And he was snapped up by his old Everton and Wales captain Kevin Ratcliffe to provide cover at Shrewsbury, before occupying a similar position at Dagenham. And Redbridge.

It's always been said that Neville Southall has ambitions to return to Goodison Park one day as manager. That may well happen. The man has proven over the years that his determination and will should never be underestimated. He's come a long way from the time when he started out as a centre-back trying to impress the likes of Crewe and Bolton (and failing to do so). And let's give words of praise to little-known Llandudno Swifts, with whom he got his first taste as a goalkeeper.

Now an MBE, awarded for his huge services to football, Southall holds the record for being the most-capped Welsh international (91), and his place in the pantheon of Goodison glory is assured. Is he the greatest Evertonian of them all? Perhaps, but one thing *is* certain – when fans put together their all-time-great Everton XI, he is the automatic choice in goal.

CHAPTER TWENTY-NINE

ANDY GRAY

EVERTON PLAYING CAREER: 1983–1985
GAMES PLAYED: 68
GOALS SCORED: 22

There have been more prolific goalscorers at Goodison than Andy Gray – his record of just 22 goals in a total of 68 appearances is hardly on the Richter scale when judged against the feats of Dixie Dean, Dave Hickson, Bob Latchford, Graeme Sharp, or even Gary Linker. He didn't have the skills of Alex Young or Duncan McKenzie, nor the natural agility of Joe Royle or Roy Vernon. So why is it that Andy Gray is one of the most revered and respected figures in the history of Everton? How is it possible that he made such a colossal mark on the club in just 18 months?

The answer lies in the fact that Gray was – indeed, remains – that rarity in football: a true hero. A man who stepped straight out of the *Roy of the Rovers* mould, and believed – always believed – that anything could be achieved by both himself and the team. He was a talisman, an icon, and his impact is still felt to this day.

But when Gray arrived in November 1983, for £250,000 from Wolves, most Evertonians despaired. Yet again, while deadly rivals Liverpool were raising the bar across Europe, the boys in blue were shopping at the bargain basement. Gray, always whole-hearted and committed, had a history of injury problems, and most believed that manager Howard Kendall was running out of ideas and hope. Everton were close to the bottom of the then first division, and were felt to be among the favourites for the dreaded drop.

But almost immediately Gray started to endear himself to the diehards. He clearly wore the shirt with pride and an incredible passion. It was as if he was born to lead the Everton line. It was as if the spirit of Dixie coursed through his Caledonian veins. He would throw his head in where most others would think twice about putting in a tentative boot. He was fearless, and a born leader. He inspired and cajoled. While Kevin Ratcliffe might have been the official captain on the pitch, here was the sort of leader that Everton hadn't had in decades. Perhaps one could go back to Bobby Collins at the start of the 1960s, but Gray never let his head drop, or those of his team-mates, and the fans took him to their hearts.

Gray had first made his mark at Dundee United, before catching the eye of Aston Villa and moving south. A further transfer to the Black Country and the old gold of Molineux saw him establish a reputation as a fearsome performer who could literally frighten defences with his strength and energy. And his arrival at Goodison coincided with the good times returning. It wasn't all smooth sailing – after being dropped against Gillingham in the FA Cup in January 1984, Gray nearly quit the club – but his impact was telling as Everton started not only to climb up the table, but also to make their mark on the domestic cups in 1984. Gray himself scored a memorable goal at Wembley in the '84 FA Cup final – memorable, because he seemingly headed the ball out of Watford goalkeeper Steve Sherwood's hands and into the net for the Blues' second goal in a 2–0 win. Over the years, Sherwood has insisted it was a foul. Gray's response is typical: 'Don't know, don't care. It's in the record books, and that's what counts!'

Gray's partnership with Graeme Sharp brought out the best in his Scottish compatriot. They were lethal. Gray's belligerence with Sharp's instinct – it was one of the most effective partnerships of the era. But Gray's influence went deeper. He defied the odds and deified the hope. Nothing was beyond his vaulting ambitions, and when Everton went into the 1984–85 season looking to build on their FA Cup success, Andy Gray once again proved his mettle.

At first he seemed to be sidelined, an injury allowed Adrian 'Inchey' Heath into the team, and his partnership with Sharp reaped rich dividends for a while. But if anyone thought Gray would kick his heals on the bench they were sorely mistaken. He grabbed his chance eagerly and ravenously when Heath himself got an injury – and the season, the team and man never looked back. Gray reveled in the growing success at the club, as he drove Everton on to championship glory and then to a first-ever European trophy, as a 3–1 European Cup Winners' Cup triumph was achieved in Rotterdam over Rapid Vienna. In the 18 months since Gray's arrival, Everton had gone from also-rans in danger of disappearing to being a formidable force. Were it not for the Hysel Stadium tragedy that same season, which led to an understandable ban on English clubs in European competitions, who knows what Everton might have gone on to achieve.

But then Kendall shook Evertonians to the core – he sold Gray in the summer of 1985 to Aston Villa (receiving just ten per cent of the £1.5 million that Villa themselves had got when they sold Gray to Wolves). The club's spiritual leader had gone.

In reality, Kendall was right – Gray couldn't hope to achieve anything else for the club. He had earned an Indian summer with Everton, but approaching 30, his best years were really behind him. The toll of so many injuries, many self-inflicted because of his braveheart style of play, finally got the better of him. He saw out his playing career with firstly Villa, then Notts County and West Brom, before finally moving back to Scotland and his first love, Rangers.

However, if he wasn't the player we all wanted to recall, that didn't stop Evertonians from hurting at his departure. His replacement, Gary Lineker, might have been a better goalscorer (he netted nearly twice as many in his one season at Goodison as Gray did in his whole Blues career) and a more rounded footballer, but he didn't have those essential Gray qualities. Somehow, you couldn't see Everton buckling to Liverpool in the 1985 FA Cup final with Gray on the pitch – but it happened without him. Everton fans mourned his transfer as if a close family member had died. His personality, charisma and sheer bloodymindedness had turned him into a hero – and life without his giant presence seemed unbearable.

Gray himself didn't see his love affair with football finishing when he hung up his boots. He rejoined Aston Villa as Ron Atkinson's assistant, before moving into television with the burgeoning Sky operation in the early 1990s. Since then he has carved out an impressive career as an inciteful, intelligent pundit, who spots tactical shifts and ebbs with an expert, practiced eye. But if Evertonians thought they were to be left with only memories of Gray to comfort them on a dull winter's afternoon at Goodison after another insipid performance, then Fate nearly threw them a curveball in 1997.

As another hugely disappointing season (1996–97) lurched towards its conclusion, manager Joe Royle left the club. Club captain Dave Watson briefly took over the managerial reins, given the task of steering an obviously rudderless club through the choppy waters of relegation. He successfully achieved this aim, but wasn't considered for the job. And the man who rapidly emerged as favourite to take the position in the summer of 1997 was . . . Andy Gray.

Talks between the man and the club had apparently become so advanced that he'd even submitted a 'wish list' of players to then chairman Peter Johnson, including Aston Villa striker Dwight Yorke, a young man whom Gray had helped guide towards becoming a major force on the Premiership. The tabloids even at one point reported Gray was within 24 hours of accepting the job. And then . . . .

It all went wrong. Gray decided to sign a new contract with Sky Sports, and fans were left wondering if he'd used the club to get a better contract out of the TV giant. Gray's stock plummeted, and he was suddenly turned from being a hero into a pariah; he was even jeered at a subsequent appearance at Goodison to cover a match – something that almost defied belief.

With the passing of the years, opinions have softened. It would now seem that Gray never used Everton for anything. He was genuinely interested in the job, and had enough faith in his own abilities to do it, for better or worse. But he would have been hampered by a distinct lack of funds, and when he realised that he couldn't built the team he wanted, understandably Gray walked away from the club he loves. Wearing his heart on his sleeve, he simply wouldn't accept doing a job that he knew was doomed to failure. And so Everton had to content themselves with a third spell in charge from Howard Kendall.

To this day, Evertonians wonder what Gray might have achieved as a manager. We can only speculate, but it would have been a rollercoaster ride. And who knows, maybe one day Andy Gray will take that job – and lead Everton back to the glory days.

'It was only 18 months and 22 goals,' recalls Gray of those playing days, 'but I certainly enjoyed myself and I hope the fans did too.'

We did, Andy, we did.

CHAPTER THIRTY

PAUL RIDEOUT

EVERTON PLAYING CAREER: 1992–1997
GAMES PLAYED: 140
GOALS SCORED: 40

Paul Rideout will always be remembered at Goodison Park for one goal and one goal only. It happened at Wembley in the 1995 FA Cup final against Manchester United. His first-half header gave Everton the trophy, rounding off not only a remarkable transformation in the fortunes of the club, but also Rideout's most successful season at Goodison, when he pocketed 16 goals, ending up as the Blues' top scorer. Those lucky enough to be at Wembley that day will forever recall how Graham Stuart hit the underside of the bar, when it seemed easier to put Matt Jackson's sweeping cross into the net, and how Rideout reacted faster than anyone in a red shirt to firmly pot the rebound. A truly glorious highlight for the striker in a career that never really took off. He should have been a contender, as the saying goes, but for various reasons, he never achieved what was expected.

In his early days, Rideout was perceived as being one of the most promising young players in the country. Many expected him to follow selection at England Schools, Youth and Under-21 levels with full international honours. But it never happened. A combination of bad luck and injuries saw him reduced to bit roles, as he lurched from club to club constantly trying to get his stalling career back on track. He started out with Swindon, for whom he scored only 8 goals in 95 appearances, before taking in Aston Villa (19 goals in 54 appearances), Italians Bari (23 goals in 99 appearances), Southampton (19 goals in 75 appearances), back to Swindon on loan (one goal in a further nine games), Notts County (one goal in 11 games) and finally, in 1991, he went to Scottish giants Glasgow Rangers.

By this point in his faltering career, Rideout was seen as a journeyman player, doomed to wander through the divisions, as his career gradually dwindled. He was virtually on the scrapheap at the age of 27 when, in August 1992, Howard Kendall decided to take a risk with him that was similar to the one he took nearly a decade previously with Andy Gray. After scoring just once in 12 games at Ibrox, Rideout headed for Goodison in a £500,000 transfer that had many Evertonians groaning with disappointment. This wasn't the sort of signing to fill them with expectation and hope for a new era.

Kendall aimed to team up the experienced and much travelled striker with Tony Cottee, hoping they would become a potent force. But it never worked out. In fact, in their first season together (1992–93) the pair only started together a paltry four times!

Things did improve in the next campaign as Kendall started to use the pairing more often, but the arrival of Mike Walker as Kendall's replacement, coupled with inevitable injury problems, restricted Rideout significantly as Everton fought a desperate battle against relegation, one that went down to the last game of the season and the famous/infamous (depending on your viewpoint) 3–2 victory over Wimbledon.

It was the arrival of Joe Royle following Walker's sacking the next season that galvanised Rideout. In the new manager's first game, at home to Liverpool, Rideout came off the bench to score the second goal in that vital 2–0 victory. From there, he didn't look back. Royle paired him with either Daniel Amokachi or Stuart, and it seemed to work rather well. His strength, and willingness to make himself available as a target man, made Rideout an important member of the team, as they clawed their way forward.

However, his injury hoodoo struck again early into the 1995–96 season, and with Duncan Ferguson (another former Ranger) raring to go, Rideout was now reduced to a bit role.

By the following year, the striker was effectively surplus to requirements, and in April 1997 he agreed to join Chinese club Huan Dao Vanguards. The fee was just £250,000, but he himself stood to make £350,00 from the adventure. But, just when it looked like Rideout had said his fond farewell to Goodison, he was recalled. Caretaker manager Dave Watson faced an injury crisis as he tried to gather the points Everton needed to avoid relegation (a familiar story at the time).

Thrown in at the deep end when Royle quit on transfer deadline day, club captain Watson was struggling with a depleted squad. In desperation, knowing that Rideout had yet to actually sign for the Chinese club, Watson hauled him back for a crucial encounter at Goodison with Spurs. Not only that, but he put the veteran into midfield. Now, Rideout had previously shown his versatility by performing in defence as well as upfront, but midfield?

If anyone doubted Watson's sanity, Rideout's performance that day was a revelation. He was the best player on view, playing with a skill, vision and focus that few believed he possessed. He was clearly the main inspiration behind a crucial 1–0 win (earned with a Gary Speed goal), and such was his command in uncharted territory that many Evertonians hoped Watson would persuade Rideout to turn his back on China, and stay on at the club in his newly discovered role of midfield maestro. How ironic that during all those years when the Everton midfield lacked creativity, the man who could have given it those qualities was right in front of everyone! The Dogs of War gained enormous attention, but Everton so patently lacked someone with a little skill to make things happen. And here was the answer.

But it wasn't to be. Rideout wasn't going to be resurrected as the new Colin Harvey, Howard Kendall and Alan Ball rolled into one.

He did complete his move to China. But the English game hadn't seen the last of him. He returned to sign for Tranmere Rovers for the 2000–01 season. And who can forget his FA Cup hat trick against a Glenn Hoddle-led Southampton in February 2001, as the Wirral side staged a remarkable comeback.

Now coaching in the United States, Rideout has hung up his boots as he approaches his 40th birthday. His career saw him travel extensively, always giving his all and scoring goals wherever he went. Not the most prolific of strikers, his 40 goals in 139 appearances for Everton represents a respectable haul, but none will stick in the memory more than the one he got at Wembley.

In many respects, he had a lot in common with Teddy Sheringham. Neither were blessed with fleetness of foot, but both made up for this with a rare footballing instinct and intelligence. In Sheringham's case, this saw him win some of the game's biggest honours, ones that sadly Rideout couldn't match. Perhaps his biggest problem – aside from constant injuries – was that he seemed to be undervalued wherever he went. No manager really seemed to understand what he could offer to a team – until Dave Watson finally gave Rideout the chance to show what he could do. Is it just possible that more enlightened managers could have encouraged Rideout to develop his skills and become as effective as did Sheringham?

Paul Rideout will not be regarded by all as a great Evertonian, even though he probably enjoyed his most fruitful spell at the club. It's there that he came into his own, and he will probably be best remembered for that. In fact, Rideout played more games for Everton than any other club in his career. And if only someone earlier on had spotted what he could do when put in the middle of the team, then things could so easily have been different. Perhaps in a parallel universe . . .

THE PRESENT DAY

One can never know where the next footballing hero will emerge. But there have been enough Everton fans in recent years who've made an major impact on the pitch. Ian Rush, Robbie Fowler, Steve McManamon, Michael Owen.

You might recognize those names. They all made their initial impact playing for . . . Liverpool. How it galls Evertonians to watch as diehard fans of the Blues are persuaded to sign for the deadly enemy. And even when the club have had genuinely promising young players, they've failed to realize that promise. From Stuart Barlow to Billy Kenny, Michael Branch to Danny Cadamarteri, there have been numerous players hailed as the Goodison riposte to those damn talents across Stanley Park. For differing reasons, all failed to make the grade. And then there's Francis Jeffers, Michael Ball and Richard Dunne – all sold when they had much to offer, although Jeffers is now back.

So, it will come as no surprise that Everton fans are both elated by, yet wary of, the emergence of Wayne Rooney. At 17, is he the real deal? So far, so good, and when was the last time that Everton had a player who created such a media frenzy? Possibly Dixie Dean – but then the media were considerably less intrusive or influential 75 years ago!

Rooney didn't just burst onto the scene, he was an atomic detonation. 'That goal' against Arsenal in 2002–03 triggered hysteria, such was the fascination and interest in a player nurtured by Everton legend Colin Harvey during his time in charge of the youth team.

Rooney has all the right attributes – strength, pace, power, accuracy and a surprising football intelligence – and as long as he's well protected by the powers-that-be at Goodison, he will surely be a major name for years to come. And as a devoted Evertonian he will be easily prised away from the club – as long as success is in his sights. Already an England international, he needs time to develop, and to be surrounded by players of equal ability. That's where David Moyes comes in.

Everton's current manager is shaping up to be the most important since Howard Kendall quit in 1987. He has already worked miracles in getting the team out of the relegation mire and within sight of the Champions League. He has clear tactical vision, a genius for getting the maximum out of any player, the respect of his squad and the confidence of his board. Regarded as one of the brightest young coaches around, he had an undistinguished playing career with Celtic and Preston, before taking over as the latter's manager, achieving so much that the bigger clubs began to come knocking. So why did he choose Everton? It felt right. The challenge is obvious, the pedigree of the club makes it such that if he does maintain the momentum of his first full season, he could take the club all the way – and write his own ticket onto the global stage. Outside of the Big Five – Manchester United, Arsenal, Chelsea, Newcastle and Liverpool – no club has more potential than Everton. Moyes knows this, and has already set about the task of taking Everton further forward than has been the case since the inception of the Premiership.

A canny dabbler in the transfer market, Moyes will not settle for second best. He'll bide his time and wait for the right man, a player who fits his pattern, rather than buy for its own sake. He does not squander money, and while he has little to spend he has made the maximum use of available funds.

What's more, Scotsman Moyes is a motivator. Never obviously demonstrative, he commands loyalty – and gives it in equal measure. He is a player's man, and shows it at every turn. Like Rooney, whom he inherited, his future at Goodison depends on being given the tools for the job, and if they are not forthcoming, he will doubtless move on.

And let nobody have any doubts about Moyes – he has a ruthless streak in him that will not countenance anything less than total dedication. That's why he has no truck with one of the club's prodigal sons, Duncan Ferguson. If ever there has been a player at Goodison who has let himself down badly it is Duncan Ferguson. To paraphrase Joe Royle, he quickly became a legend, but has failed to be the player his potential demanded. A series of injuries and suspensions, not to mention a prison sentence, have undermined his vast talent. This is allied to a seeming inability to harness and focus his talents, and it all leads to one thing: a player who will forever carry the tag 'if only' . . .

When Ferguson arrived at Everton in November 1994 on loan from Rangers, he already carried a reputation as a something of a liability. He'd been signed by Rangers from Dundee United for £4 million, but after just two goals in fourteen appearances, manager Walter Smith (who would reenter the Ferguson story at a later date) decided to send him to struggling Everton. At first he made no impact on a team adrift at the bottom of the Premiership. But all of that changed when Mike Walker was replaced as manager by Joe Royle. Himself a one-time centre-forward, Royle immediately saw the potential in Ferguson, and gave him the confidence to go out and terrorise Liverpool in a memorable 2–0 win at Goodison that kick-started the 1994–95 season for club. Another goal, the winner in a 1–0 triumph over Manchester United, sealed the giant Scotsman's stature at Goodison. In a team that had few stars, he was seen as the brightest – some even compared him to Andy Gray as the club's talismanic figure.

Fergsuon played his role in the Blues' march to FA Cup glory in 1995, although he was injured for the semi-final victory over Spurs (4–1 – possibly the team's finest performance under Royle) and only made a brief, inconsequential appearance as a substitute in the final itself, a 1–0 victory over Manchester United. The next season, all hopes for a lethal partnership with the flying Russian Andrei Kanchelskis were ruined by injuries and suspensions, while over the next couple of seasons whenever it looked like the striker would at last come good, he was again struck down by either injury or his suspect temperament.

Then in 1998, Evertonians were stunned when Peter Johnson sold Ferguson to Newcastle for £8 million in order to appease the bank. It was done behind manager Walter Smith's back, and led to such outrage that it resulted in the demise of Johnson as chairman of the club. In truth, the sale of Ferguson made sense. It was the fact that he had been transferred without Smith's consultation that was unpalatable. And, if anyone had any doubts about the logic in selling the striker, then his record of just 12 goals in 41 appearances for Newcastle should prove the point. Again, Ferguson failed to find consistency, and frustrated fans and fellow players alike. His talent was world class, but it remained largely unfulfilled.

Then in 2000, Everton committed one of their greatest follies when they bought back Ferguson for £3.75 million. It may have seemed like the return of the hero, but in reality it's been a waste of money. Since his second spell at the club started, he has scored just 14 goals, bringing his career total at Goodison to 56. And now it would seem that Moyes has grasped the nettle, believing that Ferguson might have a place in Everton folklore, but this is not backed up by the facts. Former club captain, Ferguson is now into his 30s and is in an inevitable decline. The legend looks set never to become the player.

It's hard to believe that anyone else currently at Goodison will feature prominently in *Everton Greats*. David Unsworth in two spells at the club has proved to be wholehearted, solid yet ultimately not quite the player everyone believed he might have been when he stormed into the team in 1994–95. Kevin Campell has given his all for Everton; now in his sixth season at the club, his 50-plus goals have often been crucial. Many believe that Everton have seen the best of Campbell – this has been the most settled and consistent period of his career. Now a veteran, he cannot claim to have the same hold over Evertonians as previous heroes, but one thing he has done is help bury the myth that the club is racist. He has always been accepted and encouraged.

Elsewhere, it is a case of worthy journeymen who are doing a manful job, but not players who have the streak of genius within them. Perhaps central defender Joseph Yobo will emerge as a player of genuine class – many have faith in him. And at least fellow central defender Alan Stubbs is now back with the club he idolized as a boy. But there's a belief that his best days were at Bolton and Celtic.

This is indeed not exactly a period in the Blues' history that's overly blessed with characters, although there are many players with plenty of character. But who knows, perhaps the RAM (Rooney and Moyes) will inspire the next generation of true Blue heroes.